HOW TO RAISE A HUSBAND

To Gloria—
This book would
not be without
your insight &
help. Thank you!
Tonilyn

HOW TO RAISE A HUSBAND

TONILYN HORNUNG

Conari Press

First published in 2014 by Conari Press, an imprint of
Red Wheel/Weiser, LLC
With offices at:
665 Third Street, Suite 400
San Francisco, CA 94107
www.redwheelweiser.com

ISBN: 978-1-57324-635-4

Library of Congress Cataloging-in-Publication Data available upon request.

Cover design by Jim Warner
Cover photograph © shutterstock/Vladimir Gjorgiev
Interior by Maureen Forys, Happenstance Type-O-Rama
Typeset in Neutraface Slab Text with Universe Condensed

Printed on acid-free paper in the United States of America.
EBM

10 9 8 7 6 5 4 3 2 1

The paper used in this publication meets the minimum requirements of the American National Standard for Information Sciences—Permanence of Paper for Printed Library Materials Z39.48-1992 (R1997).

For my husband:

Without you my stories would have no love, and my sentences would have no commas.

Your support has raised me to heights I never imagined possible.

P.S. I'm sorry I couldn't change your name to Han Solo.

Author's Note

Here in this book of words lies the absolute truth about marriage. This is the truth that your mother could never tell you. This is the truth your married girlfriends warned you about in secret code that sounded something like, "Whew. Marriage."

Five brave women gave me permission to poke around in the psyche of their marriages.* (My husband gave me permission to poke around in mine—after I told him to give me permission.) And these wonderful wives have allowed me to write their tales. I am forever grateful for their trust.

Some story details have been altered, but all the situations and solutions reached by these ingenious wives are absolutely true.

*All names (except mine) have been changed to protect the (mostly) innocent husbands.

The Almost Happily Married Wives and Their Husbands:

Tonilyn and Michael–Married Nine Years

Christine and Danny–Married Twelve Years

Lily and Gus–Married Eight Years

Ellen and Frank–Married Forty-One Years

Sophie and Nick–Married Nineteen Years

Chloe and Malcolm–Married Thirteen Years

Contents

"Welcome to How to Raise a Husband. *I am the husband. My beautiful bride may have written this tome, but I, in my infinite humble objectivity, plainly see that* How to Raise a Husband *exists only because of me."*

—MICHAEL, Tonilyn's husband, from the afterword

Introduction

My husband is right. (Don't tell him I said that.) He is the reason this book exists. He alone is responsible for my being able to write a whole tome about marriage, husbands, and wives, instead of writing about my love for cows that make TV commercials. But truthfully, he was not my inspiration. That honor falls to another woman . . . and a chicken club sandwich.

"I asked him to watch her for two seconds and guess what?" my girlfriend asked as I scarfed down my lunch, "I came back and he was *watching* TV, and she was trying to crawl *off* the couch! She could have fallen and really hurt herself!"

She was right.

Later that afternoon, while wondering how to make the tangy spread on that chicken sandwich, I replayed my friend's conversation in my head. How could her husband not know that he needed to actually watch his twelve-month-old and not the latest episode of *Homeland*?

And that's when it hit me—*they use* Caesar salad dressing *on their sandwich!* Okay but right after that—*not only did my dear friend have a child to raise, but she had a husband to raise as well.* I started thinking, "Do all wives feel like they are raising their husbands? Wow. Someone should write a book about that." And I promptly went on dreaming about drowning my next chicken sandwich in Caesar salad dressing.

Weeks later the title *How to Raise a Husband* popped into my head, and it occurred to me that, as a wife and a writer, *I* could write a book about wives and husbands. (Admittedly, I can be a little slow sometimes. Like the time when I thought Alaska was an island. Seriously, it's a simple mistake to make! I mean, it's always floating in the water next to Hawaii on the map.)

Since I didn't have the resources, knowledge, or enough ballpoint pens to take a nationwide poll, I asked wives I knew if they felt like they had ever "raised" their husbands during their marriage. Each and every one answered a resounding, "Yes."

So it turns out we wives and husbands are not alone in this marriage thing. I've interviewed some other wives and will share their stories along with mine. They have allowed me to be their voice and tell their tales—some in the face of opposition from their husbands, and some with their husbands thinking they've been working on a nonspecific "girl" project which I'm sure, in their world, involves pillow-fighting and a *Grease* sing-along.

Before you turn to the opening section, you should know that this book does not make a mockery of men or marriage. (Perhaps a little light poking fun at, but not a full-on poke. Those hurt.) This is not a book about stupid husbands and smart wives. This is (mostly) not a book about incapable husbands unable to find the ketchup on the second shelf of the refrigerator hidden behind the eggs. This is definitely not a book about cows and TV commercials. This is a book about real relationships and real couples trying their best to stay grounded and loving.

Because let's face it . . .

We all need to be raised up now and then.

And sometimes we need to be shown where the ketchup bottle has been hiding.

PART I

The Pre-Husbandraic Ages

Before They Were Husbands

CHAPTER 1

The Thrill of the Chase

How to get your boyfriend to come when you call

Tonilyn and Michael

My boyfriend doesn't come when I call.

It's strange. What boyfriend wouldn't want to respond to my siren-like calls of "HEY YOU!" echoing down the hall? There must be something wrong with his hearing. At first when I posed this theory to myself, it seemed unlikely. Michael can hear his phone ring from the next room, and he can make out the pizza guy's knock from the backyard. But then after watching *Star Wars* for the thirty-ninth time together, it finally hit me—the television.

My boyfriend's television set is turned up so loud it shakes the walls of the house and the brain inside my head. Maybe he really can't hear the subtle explosion of the Death Star. Maybe he has trouble making out Red Leader telling the X-Wing squadron he'd just lost his starboard engine. It's possible. This would certainly explain why I need earplugs to watch a movie with him.

Being the clever and fair-minded girlfriend that I am, I decided to conduct a little hearing test of my own. I wouldn't want to falsely accuse Michael of not listening to me if he couldn't, in fact, listen to me. So, I came up with what I thought was a foolproof test of my boyfriend's hearing.

I now know that at a distance of twenty feet, separated by an entire room, my boyfriend can make out whispered key words and phrases such as "dinner is ready," "the Dallas Cowboys," or "Lando Calrissian." When I speak these magic words, my boyfriend responds immediately, bounding into whatever room I happen to be in.

"Did you call me?"

His hearing is fine. Why then doesn't he come when I call?

Shouting his name doesn't work. There was a time I tried silkily shouting "Michael" lovingly and beautifully through the house after him. My light soprano-like trills echoed down the hall like Snow White singing into her wishing well. How is it then that my handsome prince of a boyfriend did not mount a dignified steed and immediately ride to my rescue? The only explanation: All the dignified steeds had been rented that day.

For a week or so, I tried disguising my voice and shouting a manly, staccato "HEY!" from his bedroom to the living room. I hoped I might be mistaken for one of his male roommates. Michael responds to their manly "HEY!" cries regarding pizza and socks much quicker than my more womanly bellows about date night and the guy at work who upset me. No matter how I tried to alter my voice, I couldn't get it right. I sounded like a cold-ridden version of Miss Piggy.

I've tried calling his name lovingly. I've tried calling his name urgently. I've tried calling him names. Nothing. I am shouting into The Darkness where tiny bathroom objects (like my elastic ponytail holders) and socks from the dryer are pulled in to disappear forever. My voice is lost in the cavernous Void.

What if it were an honest-to-God emergency? What if I were sitting in the living room and the window valance suddenly fell on top of me?! What if I were trapped with only mere seconds before the purple window treatment cut off my much needed air supply? Just to be on the safe side, along with hollering for Michael to come and rescue me, I think I'd also cry out for Robert Downey Jr. to come save me. I figure Mr. Jr. is just as likely to hear my wails and rescue me as my boyfriend is. (And autograph my *Weird Science* poster.)

It would be so much easier for me if I could place this issue high upon the Trivial Things in a Relationship shelf. Other issues on this shelf include endearing dating quirks like making sure I return his CDs to their original cases. For some reason it's important to Michael that his CDs be in the matching case. (My CDs tend to migrate from non-matching case to non-matching case, so my collection is full of surprises.) Or even smaller quirks like my having to place Michael's dental floss back the way I found it—behind the bathroom faucet, label side against the wall, like it's awaiting execution—lest I receive a long lecture regarding the proper placement of his things.

I can't seem to reach the shelf with this selective hearing foible.

"Michael!"

In the silence, there is hope. For every scream that escapes my throat, I wonder if this will be the one that is answered.

When I was a kid, thunderstorms were not my favorite thing. (I liked them slightly more than the evil Skeksis from *The Dark Crystal.*) I would lie awake in bed thinking that this next lightning strike would bring about my instant demise. In an effort to allay my fears, my dad taught me how to "count the storm." I'd see the lightning brighten up my room, and then I'd start counting to ten, hoping I would reach past five. The higher I could count, the farther away the storm would be, and the safer I would feel. Once safely past the number five, I could breathe a sigh of relief. And happily return to my dreams of Han Solo.

This counting system worked so well as a child that I decided to employ it with my boyfriend. After my beautiful operatic-like scream for Michael, I count. *One, two, three, four, five, six, seven, eight, nine, ten. . . .* In this case, however, the opposite rings true—the higher I count, the worse I feel.

Still, giddy with anticipation, I wait. My stomach has that all-too-familiar excited feeling that it gets the night before the Black Friday Macy's sale.

Ears pricked, I listen for an answer. I wait to hear a loving, "WHAT?!" ring back down the hall. Or better yet, maybe my strapping young fellow will stop buying *Star Wars* action figures on eBay long enough to come see what I need.

Or not.

In the silence, there is also silence. I know my boyfriend can hear me. I know he is choosing not to respond. I know he is not choosing me.

"Why don't you come when I call?"

I hear the question in my head daily, but I can't seem to make my mouth form the words. It seems more like a question for my dog than my boyfriend. This would be why I haven't asked him—my boyfriend, not my dog. I know why my dog doesn't come when I call him—I'm not made of Milk-Bones. I don't know why my boyfriend won't come—but I'm afraid to ask and I'm afraid of his answer.

When Michael calls for me, I answer. I stop whatever it is that I'm doing because he is more important than my *Project Runway* watching and more important than Oreo eating—barely. I want him to know this. I want him to know that I'm there when he needs me—even if it's only to approve his t-shirt choice for the day. I come when he calls. Why doesn't he come when I call?

"HEY, Michael!"

One, two, three, four, five, six, seven, eight, nine, ten . . .

Nothing.

Walking down the hall in search of my wandering boyfriend signals my defeat. I trudge down the corridor trying to hide my disappointment.

I am chasing him.

I want to be chased.

Michael forgets to talk to me. Well, really it's not that he forgets to talk to me—it's that he forgets to listen to me. He forgets to ask about my day. He forgets to ask my opinion. He forgets. Enough that I notice. And that's when the yelling down the hall starts.

I'm calling so that I can share my day, or the random thought I had, or how I dreamt about Chewbacca speaking German again. I dream of a world where Michael hangs on my every word. (Or at least ten out of every 12,564 of them.)

"How come you never come when I call?" I practiced on my dog and finally got the nerve to say it to my boyfriend.

"What do you mean?"

"I mean, how come when I yell your name, so I can tell you something exciting and interesting, you don't respond?"

"I'm doing stuff," he answered while still staring at the computer screen, "I can't break my concentration like that. I have to get to a stopping point . . ." His voice trailed off . . .

A stopping point? Isn't a stopping point a stopping point? His stopping point always seems to be sometime next week. But now since we've touched on the subject, maybe he'll make more of an effort to answer.

"Michael!"

One, two, three, four, five, six, seven, eight, nine, ten . . .

Or not.

Are my conversational skills that mundane? I try to introduce subjects that interest both of us. Appealing subjects like why *The Empire Strikes Back* is the best of the original trilogy or boobs. I love *Star Wars*, and I have boobs. I can't think of a more winning combination than that for a guy.

Like a clever Victorian hostess, I add these subjects on at the end of my monologue about why I cried in traffic yesterday and why the lady who yelled at her dogs in the park made me so mad. My choice of closing topics ends our conversation with a brilliant discussion that leaves us laughing. I feel valued. I always leave my audience wanting more. So, why then won't he come when I call?

Ah.

I see my mistake.

"Michael! *The Empire Strikes Back* is on . . ."

It would seem that my boyfriend responds best to certain specific stimuli.

"Did you call me?"

"Yeah. But before we watch, let me tell you about the crazy dream I had last night . . ."

CHAPTER 2

Race to the Rings

How to survive pressure from your partner

Christine and Danny

The day I never imagined would happen is happening. My wedding day. I never imagined it would happen because I never imagined it would happen. Too bad my fiancé has already set the date, sent out our wedding invitations, and gone on our honeymoon. I didn't imagine this.

Love has many different speeds, and Danny's is set on warp drive. My fiancé is super excited to tie the knot. All the bridal magazines Danny has given me tell me that this is a good thing. According to the latest issue of *Today's Bride*, along with lemon wedding cake being the hip new thing, wedding planning can actually make a man nervous. This is something I have yet to experience, so I'll take *Today's Bride* at its word. Why would the magazine lie about men or cake?

Getting married was never a subject Danny avoided—like one article *Today's Bride* explores, "Marriage: A Subject Men Avoid." The article goes on to discuss how some impatient girlfriends give their boyfriends marital ultimatums or deviously tape tiny photos of diamond rings to their man's deodorant in an effort to encourage a walk down the aisle. I never had to drop one single marital hint.

Danny was ready.

So was I. I thought.

"Christine, when are we setting the date?"

"I . . ."

"Christine, when are we picking the church?"

"I . . ."

"Christine, when are we going to register?"

"I . . ."

"Christine, when are we going to have our engagement party?"

"I . . ."

A plate of cooked vegetables freaks out my fiancé more than planning our wedding. If only Danny could eat his green beans with as much speed and gusto as he peruses wedding invitation fonts.

While I'm happily envisioning what our font might look like, Danny is asking, "How about this one," waiting for me to give him a final verdict. (I didn't even know there was a font called Plantagenet Cherokee.) I'm not ready to decide. I'm ready to dream!

Unlike the other nine-year-olds in my fourth-grade class, I never dreamt about my big day in puff paint, magazine clippings, and giggles. Why go through the hassle of planning a Hawaiian-themed wedding only to discover I'm not going to marry Magnum P.I.? I decided I'd start fantasizing once I met my fiancé. So, now I've met my fiancé. (*Yay!*) I'm officially ready to start *dreaming*! (*Yay!*) Danny is ready to start *deciding*. (*Boo.*) His usual Internet searches have changed from "Iron Man vs. Agent Mulder" to "Baseball-shaped groom's cake" and "Iron Man boutonniere." Our upcoming nuptials have lit a fire under Danny like I've never seen. The problem is I may suffocate from all the smoke. How am I going to survive all of this Partner Pressure?

In my estimation, Partner Pressure is a much more intense and slightly less subtle version of peer pressure. Like every straight-haired girl of the 1980s, I too experienced peer pressure in school. This stress took the form of trying to make my bangs defy gravity. It was nothing a teasing comb and massive amounts of Salon Selectives hairspray couldn't fix. However, taller bangs didn't prepare me for the kind of stress a bride-to-be can feel while trying to be a bride.

Today's Bride hinted that a bride can feel massive amounts of pressure while planning a wedding. Strangely, the article "Pressure a Bride Can Feel," alluded more to the bride's immediate family as a cause of tension. The article went on to say that sometimes even a mother-in-law can step in and give her opinion more freely than is comfortable, thus causing difficulty. I have yet to find an article on the groom creating unwanted anxiety and dizziness.

I've never been a person to make fast decisions. I like to feel things out. I like to take the problem home and sleep on it. My fiancé, on the other hand, knows what he wants and he wants it now—much like how he knew he wanted me.

In the middle of a party, a slightly drunken version of my now fiancé professed his undying love for me and our unborn children. We'd only been friends for a few of months, so this came as quite the campfire confession. It might have even been romantic except for the part where he was drunk. With lightning speed, Danny moved from the more accepted "Boy this fire sure is hot," and "Would you like another marshmallow?" campfire small talk to confessing that I was his soul mate with pretty eyes.

This was a lot of information to throw at a girl! I needed time to process. I needed to take that revelatory news home and sleep on it. Cuddle with it. Put it under my pillow—for a year. It took me one whole year before we went out on an official date.

All right, it could be I'm a little slow to process things. But I can *make* decisions. On the spot, I can decide what dessert to eat. I can decide what color pants to wear. I can decide to marry my boyfriend. Still there are some instances when I need that extra little space to mull it over. *Today's Bride* says it's all right to weigh my bridal decisions carefully—to take my time while deciding on chair cover colors. I wish my fiancé thought the same thing.

"Christine, we really need to set a date."

"Honey, can't we just enjoy being engaged?"

Confusion spread across his face—like I'd just taken away his Happy Meal and offered him a vegetable stir-fry.

"Sure we can."

Ah, sweet relief.

"But we really need to set a date."

"We really need to set a date," has become the bane of my conversational existence. I can't have a conversation that doesn't begin or end with those six little words and a woozy feeling.

"Christine, we really need to set a date. What's for dinner?"

"Christine, we really need to set a date. Are we going out tonight?"

"Christine, which *Iron Man* movie are you in the mood for? We really need to set a date."

Every time the subject is broached, my face turns into a frozen mask (much like Iron Man's), and I stand there stiff and tense. Since Danny and I took so long to get to our first official date, maybe he's afraid I'll never make a wedding decision. It's a possible reason why he's in such a hurry to walk down the . . . ahem . . . *run* down the aisle. I want to give him the answer he so needs to hear. But I'd really like to take a second to get used to the weight of the engagement ring on my finger first.

"Christine, we really need to set a date."

"Honey, we've only been engaged two weeks," I tried reasoning.

Danny looked confused.

I feel like my fiancé isn't really listening to me. This could be due to the fact that he's not really listening to me.

I can hear the voice inside my head telling me to just set the date. *Christine . . . set the date. It's not that hard.* (Funny, that voice sounds a lot like Danny's.) If I set the date, maybe Danny would feel more reassured and then the rest of the planning process would slow down to a mild jog. Being married is about compromise, right?

"All right, Honey, how about June 9?"

"Great! I'll call my family."

Done.

Danny had his date. The planning would slow down from here on out. I guess maybe that wasn't as bad as I thought.

"Christine, when are we going to pick the venue?"

It was as bad as I thought.

Not even five minutes to get my scrapbooking scissors out to begin cutting out my bridal dreams.

Even though I had never fantasized about my wedding day, I did imagine how I'd feel planning it. I envisioned my fiancé and me blissfully working together, happily orchestrating the best day of our lives. Nowhere did I see my groom-to-be presenting me with the scariest thing I've ever seen—a checklist. Through this whole process my mental list has simply read, "Enjoy." I didn't see that anywhere on *his* list.

Although *Today's Bride* encourages a separate bride and groom checklist, I don't think the author of the article expected my Groomzilla to be handling both lists. I'm now conditioned to feel an immediate sense of dread when I see the list coming out. When the checklist emerges, I know the questions and faintness are to follow.

My married life is flashing before my eyes. Is this engagement pressure just the beginning? Once we're married, will Danny continue to bring out his list of decisions that I have to make? Will he suddenly have a decorators checklist? A baby-making checklist?

"Christine, when are we going to pick the venue?"

Danny, when are you going to stop asking me questions?!

I want to make my fiancé happy. I do. This is why I haven't told him to back off yet.

It was no secret that the next big checkmark Danny wanted to earn for his list was crossing off our wedding venue. Thank goodness. This was an easy one because I thought it would be great if we could be married in the same Catholic church where my parents were married. But more than the venue picking, I was super excited to finally meet with the priest.

One thing I *had* dreamt about was standing at the altar listening to the priest ask, "Do you take this man to be your husband?" I was going to be able to finally cross something off two of my own lists: my wedding list and my Good Catholic Girl list! (See, I have lists, too.) I'd already checked off four of the sacraments off my Good Catholic Girl list, and this would be number five.

Getting married will immediately reduce my list of sacraments from seven to six. One of the sacraments is Holy Orders, and since Danny has proposed, this means it's unlikely I'll be taking the veil anytime soon. That only leaves one sacrament (Anointing of the Sick) unchecked, and hopefully that one will take a long time to get to—unless Danny gives me a heart attack with all the rushed planning.

I was so excited to get one of my wedding dreams met! We just needed to meet with the priest and make it official. I could give Danny his much-needed checkmark, and I could begin dreaming about my wedding! This one would be a piece of cake. Call it a wedding gift.

My gift could not be delivered.

This time it was the priest (not me) slowing down my fiancé's checklist. Another one of the few dreams I'd had the time to conjure up was our last song. I knew in my heart what song must be played at the end of the ceremony. The priest refused. He would not play "Don't Stop Believin'" as our recessional. This pop song couldn't be found in the church hymnal along with "On Eagle's Wings" and "One Bread, One Body," so it couldn't be used. Father Sean was surprised when this good little Catholic girl explained how she wouldn't be needing his marital services. Possibly at the peril of my immortal soul, I still wasn't willing to compromise—not even to give Danny his red checkmark.

In my head I could hear Danny saying, "Christine, we have to decide . . .," and I wanted to grab his list, rip it up, throw it out onto the sidewalk, and hope a small bird could use it for a nest.

Throughout this whole race to the rings, I had settled for what would make my fiancé feel happy and safe. Even though I was bothered, in most cases I decided it was all right. I had given up on things that were slightly important to me, but so much more important to him. I tried to match Danny's fast pace and quick decision making because it seemed so crucial for his peace of mind. But I wanted my big hair ballad *and* my Catholic priest. This was one thing on which I could not simply settle; it was too important to me.

Before Danny could pull out his list, I said, "I want a Catholic priest." The end. Well, he wanted me to make final decisions, so I gave him one.

At my own pace, I researched priests online. I finally found one willing to give me my dream wedding—one who enjoyed 1980s power ballads.

Planning a wedding can be a challenge. At least that's what the *Today's Bride* article entitled "Planning a Wedding Can Be a Challenge" argues. The author encourages the bride to be open to compromise while sticking to her guns—a concept I wholeheartedly agree with, which is why I'm happy to watch Danny run down that aisle on our wedding day. Once he gets to that altar, though, he's going to have to wait—for me. I'm going to take my own sweet time breathing in every second while I *slowly* make my way down that long center aisle to meet him.

CHAPTER 3

My Favorite Person

How to stay cool in a heated discussion

Lily and Gus

My simple question, "Why can't you be nicer?" opened a huge can of resentment and anger. The most grievous of my wrongdoings being, "Lily, you're not listening." Which is curious, because I distinctly heard my boyfriend say that.

"Why do you care what I do?" Gus ranted on, "You're not listening . . ."

I *was* listening.

I was also thinking.

Contrary to popular belief, I can do both.

I was silently calculating the probability of my survival if I was to jump out of this moving car á la Harrison Ford in *Raiders of the Lost Ark*. Sadly, I'd left my bullwhip and fedora at home—both of which were necessary components for my plan to succeed. I'd also missed the day they taught Jumping Out of Cars in my Stage Combat class. I was stuck.

I'd unwittingly let the ghosts out of the Ark of the Covenant on this ride home. (Not the beautiful ones, but the ugly skeleton-looking ones accompanied by the creepy music.) I could only hope that the evil looks my boyfriend was shooting my way wouldn't melt my face off like Toht's at the end of *Raiders*. I'm not sure my complexion could recover. No amount of concealer could conceal that.

"I just don't understand why you can't simply be nicer to him," I pleaded.

"You weren't even there," Gus accused, his frustration rising. "You just assume I'm the asshole."

I couldn't contradict my boyfriend on that one. He was absolutely correct. I wasn't there. But I didn't have to be there to know what happened. All I had to do was know my boyfriend.

Gus can be impolite. Not to everyone—just people. Well, those people he doesn't like. In his defense, he likes most people just fine.

Usually, Gus is a teddy bear of a man weeping at Hallmark commercials and Woody Allen movies, but when Gus doesn't like a person, he won't waste his time. There are no polite smiles. There are no mumbled "Hellos." There's only silence—an obvious silence at that.

How is that right? How is that a civil and nice way to behave—walking around ignoring people? I feel uncomfortable in my boyfriend's presence and sorry for the person he's ignoring. Not to mention, it's embarrassing. It particularly embarrasses *me*—especially when I'm around.

I try to make up for Gus' coldness by being overly polite to the person Gus is bothered by. There are a lot of unnecessary smiles and uber-courteous pleasantries exchanged such as, "How is your day?" or "Things are going well, wouldn't you say?" or better yet, "I love that sweater."

Part of me loves that Gus feels confident enough to be himself, but another part of me wishes he could be less of himself and more like me when we're working together. I feel I shouldn't have to explain to my actor boyfriend that being a performer in a show means you *make an effort* to get along with the other performers—even if you don't like them. It's basic law number three on the list of Unwritten Actor Laws. This law follows closely behind Law One: "Memorize Your Lines," and Law Two: "Know All Lyrics to All Stephen Sondheim Musicals." It's just what you do.

There is no time in a two-week rehearsal process for uncivil behavior. A cold, unfriendly attitude will bring cast morale down faster than announcing that Charlie Sheen will be taking over the lead role. My boyfriend needs to be *nice* to the Annoying Actor Guy who is annoying him.

"Why can't you simply say 'Hi' to him?" I pleaded.

"Will you please listen to my side instead of instantly taking his? You are not listening!"

Again, I heard him say that.

I'll not deny that Gus is right regarding Annoying Actor Guy. Annoying Actor Guy is annoying. Anytime the director asks AAG to move a set piece, AAG is all of a sudden completely inept. All heavy lifting, prop moving, and ancillary walking sends him down a path of not-so-quiet whining.

I've found that the best way to deal with actors of this caliber is to just be polite and move on. I've tried explaining to my boyfriend that "being friends" and "being friendly" are two different things, but it doesn't make a difference. Gus becomes a cold gust of air passing AAG in the wings. I can see it. I can feel it. It makes me shiver, and I never seem to have a sweater.

"I still don't understand why you can't just be nice. Can't you do it for me?"

"You're not listening to a word . . ."

I wish that, instead of my boyfriend accusing me of faulty hearing, he would listen to what *I'm* saying, because I'm the one making sense here. Honestly, I'm not against Gus' behavoir. I'd just like him to stop doing it.

A few of our friends have already approached me, asking, "Why doesn't Gus ever say 'Hello' to him?" If our friends have noticed, then it's just a matter of time until AAG notices, and worse yet, the entire cast. It feels like everyone is talking behind our backs.

I'm afraid I'll eventually be shunned. Soon the costume department will provide me with a giant felt "A" that I shall be forced to wear across my chest at rehearsals. Not for "Adultery," but for "Annoying."

"The whole cast knows you don't like him," I said pointedly.

Gus would now see reason.

"What do I care if the whole cast knows?!" Gus countered.

Maybe I could still jump out of the car.

My face flushed. Gus would certainly notice that. Let him. This was ridiculous! His behavior was making me sick. Why wouldn't he just suck it up and be nice? If not for himself—for me?

"I don't understand why you can't be nice!" I shot back.

"You're not me!"

"Wha . . .? Yes, I . . ."

Huh.

He was right: I'm not him. I had no response.

"In case you're wondering, you rarely take my side," Gus continued. "Please, all I'm asking you to do is listen."

The air in the car became still. I could hear the radio's muffled chatter over the motor. I sat quietly, and thought about what he was saying.

Had Gus actually said something profound with "You're not me"? Did he, in fact, mean that we were two different people—with two different approaches to life? That perhaps my point of view may not be the right one for Gus?

I wanted to contradict him.

I wanted to tell Gus he was wrong.

I wanted to tell him that of course he's my favorite person, and of course I always take his side because that's what a good girlfriend does, but I couldn't. In my effort to make him listen to me, we were not hearing *each other.* The whole time I was talking and trying to make him hear *my point,* I hadn't stopped to consider how he was feeling. He was right: I hadn't been listening.

Gus added, "You know you're my favorite person. I'm supposed to be yours."

The heavy stillness in the car settled on my shoulders.

"You're right," I said softly.

We pulled into the driveway and stayed in the car. I listened to him talk about AAG and didn't say a word. There were times I wanted to jump in, but I didn't. There were times I thought my opinion could fix the whole situation instantly, but still I held my tongue. I didn't agree or disagree—all I did was listen.

Gus calmed down the more he talked, and I tried my best to give my boyfriend space to be who he was. Later maybe I would suggest ways to help, but right now was not the time. Right now I needed to listen to my favorite person talk about his day.

I don't think I'm going to change my opinion on this point, but I don't think I have to. Listening doesn't mean I have to agree or disagree, it just means I have to listen. That's one note I can take and put in the "Relationship with Gus" file. My boyfriend just wants to be heard. I hear that. Maybe we can both learn to listen to each other.

"Now, what was it you were saying?" Gus asked after he'd finished.

Or one of us can.

It's a start.

CHAPTER 4

Testing the Tattooed Waters

How to apply a fake tattoo and test your new boyfriend's staying power

Sophie and Nick

"Is that *real*?" Nick asked, trying to fake a casual tone. Nick was not good at faking a casual tone. I was learning a lot tonight.

"Yes . . . it's . . . um . . .real."

Technically I wasn't lying: It was a *real* tattoo. It just wasn't a real *permanent* tattoo. It was a real phony stick-on. Nick was looking at my shoulder like I had suddenly contracted the plague. I figured Nick would be especially relieved when I told him the good news—that my tattoo had been applied with a kitchen sponge and water instead of a tiny scraping drill and permanent ink. I'll admit it: I'm kind of trying Nick on along with this tattoo.

"You're sure that's real?" Nick wasn't totally convinced. He sat next to me sipping his merlot and trying to compose himself. I could see him struggling to grasp this new piece of information about his new girlfriend.

I wasn't sure what kind of reaction I'd get, but the flummoxed expression on Nick's face gave away everything. One little stick-on rose had thrown him for a loop. What kind of girl was I if I had a tattoo? Ten bucks says Nick was now wondering where I hid my leather biker jacket and my Harley—and my burly, bearded Hells Angel boyfriend.

The moment my orange shirt slid off my shoulder, all of Nick's "nice-girl" beliefs about me were shattered. Even though he wasn't running away screaming in tattooed-terror, I did see him eyeing the door for a possible quick escape. Nick was at a loss. Could he ever fall for this possible Harley-riding wild child? I need to know. I need to know because I've fallen for him. I'm totally head-over-rhinestone-stilettos for Nick and his predictable khakis. I need to know if I'm getting the boot now vs. later. I need to know before I fall any farther.

It was on our second date that I knew. I knew I had met the man I wanted to marry. Something soft inside just said, "This is him," and I believed it. But he and I had only known each other a short while—hence the little tests here and there.

I know it might not be totally fair for me to be testing him, but I've certainly learned a lot about my khaki-wearing boyfriend with this quicker pop-quiz method. Not only have I discovered that Nick's whole CD collection is alphabetically organized and on index cards, but I've also found out that Nick has a whole laundering process that any dry cleaning establishment would envy. His work shirts are so stiff we could have played Around the World Ping-Pong on them. What I found curious (after a little girlfriend apartment snooping) was that Nick doesn't own so much as a bottle of starch or an ironing board.

"Where do you get your shirts dry-cleaned? They look so great." Sneaky—I know.

"Um . . . I don't have a dry cleaner . . ."

What *was* his secret?

His mother.

My twenty-six-year-old boyfriend made special weekly trips to Mom's to bring her his shirts so that she could have the privilege of pressing and starching them. Test Number One had begun.

Nick had not met a woman who was going to spend the rest of her life ironing. No way was I going to take over his mother's role. And more to the point—I don't iron. (One of my prerequisites for buying pants is whether or not they are that fancy no-wrinkle type.) I don't iron my own clothes, so why would I iron his?

I thought it best to have a little adult heart-to-heart about his laundering choice.

"You're a grown man living in your own place, and your mother does your ironing?"

Although he was slightly surprised at my conversation topic, I could tell by the expression on his face that he was following. "I think it's time for you to take care of yourself."

Maybe he wanted to show me he was mature. Maybe he wanted to show me he was ready to take constructive criticism. What he did show me was that he could iron.

Test Number One passed with flying colors! Now would Nick pass this tattoo test too?

"So, that's real?" Nick and his starched shirt asked.

The man I am going to marry blatantly stared at my shoulder, his mouth agape. For a second, I felt a little devious, but then I remembered this tattoo test was as much for Nick as it was for me.

I want to get a tattoo—eventually. I have a whole file folder of possible designs, but I sense the true commitment of the whole occasion, so I'm still taking my time. I'd hate to end up with a pink Pegasus that I love now, only to regret it staring at me from my ankle two years later. I know better. I know not to dive straight into the deep end—like that time in 1987 when I decided that I needed my hair to look like Rod Stewart's. I thought maybe my scissors and I had pulled it off until my mom said, "Well, I guess you won't do that again." My thick brunette locks couldn't do The Rod, but a valuable lesson was learned as I waited long slow months for the disaster to grow out: Sometimes it's best not to jump in.

My instinct might be to dive, but my experience has taught me otherwise. I need to try things out first in a non-permanent fashion—like trying on a new dress. The dress might look sensational hanging there under the buzzing fluorescents, but then back in the dressing room, it becomes something your high school nemesis dreamed you'd wear to the prom. Always try it on first—a good motto under any circumstances.

"So, it's real. It is real, right?" Nick couldn't take his eyes off me—my shoulder, that is.

"It looks real, doesn't it?" Nick could sense that my answer was evasive, but the fear of it being a real tattoo took over. I could see tiny beads of sweat appearing on his upper lip.

I know myself better than Nick does, and I know I can be a changeable challenge. This is not to say I'm moody. I don't change my feelings like I change my shoes. It's not that. I change my appearance—a lot.

One day I might come home with purple hair. One day I might come home with a tattoo. I want to know that Nick is going to be all right with that. I want to know that Nick is going to be all right with who I am. My leaving the house as a brunette and coming home as a blonde could be disconcerting—not to mention a little hair-raising—if you're not used to it. I doubt Nick is used to it. The color scheme of his clothing ensemble hasn't changed in the two weeks we've been dating. It has varied from beige to a lighter shade of beige.

The type of girl he is used to dating is the same—beige and predictable. They're nothing like me. Not even close. They're rule-following nice girls with their perfect little black flats to go with their perfect little slightly-below-the-knee khaki skirts. I can guarantee that none of these girls would ever entertain the idea of a tattoo, let alone reduce themselves to putting on a stick-on. (I bet they all love to iron too.) Nick's exes were safe. I was not.

Could he really love me for me? Would he wonder where I hid my little black flats in the back of my closet?

"Really? That's really real?" Nick asked again.

I had a feeling Nick might not be quite as easygoing as he presented himself. It's not that he'd been misrepresenting himself, it's just that he hadn't been faced with anything that challenged his belief system. Enter me and my tattoo. I'm learning a lot about Nick in this tattooed portion of the evening. For instance:

- Nick is horrible at hiding his shock and confusion.
- Nick is a terrible liar.
- Nick does not like tattoos.
- Nick likes my shirt to fall off my shoulder.

All good things to know.

"So, did that . . . hurt?" Nick asked, again studying my shoulder.

I could see him contemplating what this meant. I could sense the "What am I going to tell my mom about this girl" confusion. I had taken Nick completely out of his comfort zone. His lips were pursed, and he kept tapping his wineglass in some sort of Morse code SOS.

But he didn't run.

He didn't excuse himself by explaining to me how he had to clean his pool early the next morning. (When he doesn't have a pool.) He stayed—uncomfortable and awkward as it was for him. I had lured him out of his safe place and into choppy tattooed waters, but still he stayed.

"Well," after a big gulp of wine I began, "it's not a real tattoo in the sense that it's a real tattoo . . ."

Nick stared.

"It's real in the sense that it's on my shoulder. But it's a stick-on."

Nick's huge exhale let loose all the tension he'd thought he'd been so cleverly covering. He was relieved.

"I do want to get one someday though . . ." I added.

Nick took a quick inhale and shrugged his understanding.

Obviously he wasn't thrilled, but he never ran for the door. He never asked me where I kept my Harley either. Maybe we could work.

Nick's eyes went from staring at my tattoo to staring at me.

The rest of the night Nick stayed right next to me and laughed (albeit nervously) about my thorny rose tattoo. I suggested that perhaps we get matching tattoos, but I don't think he was on board with that plan. It did seem, however, that he was totally on board with us.

Test passed.

I'm relieved that Nick isn't going to go rummaging through my closet for some black flats and safe starched khaki pants. I am free to be me. I can wear my red platforms and wrinkled shirts anytime I want. (Unless I ask Nick to iron them.) So, I'm thinking of graduating Nick to the next level—test free. Even though I haven't settled on a tattoo, I have settled on a husband.

I'm wondering though, is now a good time to tell my future husband about my future nose-piercing?

CHAPTER 5

An Imperfect Match

How to deal with a competitive boyfriend and win

Ellen and Frank

"Here's your racquet. You hold it like this . . ."

Frank handed me the tennis racquet, coldly adjusted my fingers, and walked with a steely expression over to the other side of the net. Um, where was my patient, loving instructor? Where were my soft caresses? When was Romantic Tennis Time going to start?

Across the net, my boyfriend stood in his cute tennis shorts unsmiling and unfriendly. There was no laughter. There was no fun. There were only precise instructions. I figured I'd give him the benefit of the doubt here. Perhaps he was just eager to get the game going and start the fun, because the fun hadn't started during the instruction-giving portion of our field day. This was weird.

In the past I've dated more "active" guys—like the guy on the baseball team. Or the guy on the basketball team. Or the guy on the football team. (According to the football jock, I have quite the passing arm.) I liked going out with all these outdoorsy boys because I'm a more outdoorsy kind of girl.

But there were times when these competition junkies were too much. Not only were they crazy competitive in their chosen athletic field, but this energy seeped into our conversations. It seemed silly to me to argue about which ice cream flavor was best or who was better at fishing. Last time I checked, fishing was a noncompetitive sport and all ice cream flavors are best—that one's a no brainer.

Arguing makes me nervous anyway. When I hear the heated tone ramp up, my mind turns to Jell-O. I can't manage to say anything coherent. It's a terrible condition—Jell-O Mind. All those sporty boys lost way too many points picking romantic afternoon fights.

Luckily, this is where my Frank scores major points. His tally is ever on the rise, because now I'm in fact dating a man with a brain. That he uses. To be smart. I've never dated a brainiac. It's not like Frank spends all our time together quoting Newton or other dead brainy guys. We find time for lots of fun indoor activities that don't involve talking. (Don't tell my dad.)

What I love about Frank is that he loves me more than football, or baseball, or basketball. Frank and I are prefect together—indoors. But after six months inside the outside girl in me is screaming for a little sun. I'd love to find something we can do together out of doors, because I'm missing my baby oil/sunscreen combo—just a little.

I guess my new, smart boyfriend understood that when he suggested that we play tennis together. (Again, Frank keeps racking up the boyfriend points.) A tennis match! What could be more perfect? Frank loves playing tennis, so here's something we could do outside together!

I liked this outdoorsy idea much better than Frank's recent suggestions of learning to play more indoors games like Risk and Diplomacy. I don't really get the *risk* involved, and I'm not sure how *diplomatic* I'm going to be when I have no idea what kind of "bored" game I'm playing.

Playing tennis together was a great idea! I'd never played tennis, but my boyfriend says I'm "sporty," so I figured I could figure it out.

I envisioned a perfect tennis court built for two with Frank patiently showing me how to play. The two of us would laugh while the sun shone warmly down upon us. I just knew that the day was going to be amazing. We would be the perfect couple on and off the court. Afterward we would go for ice cream and talk about smart things until the sun rose—or at least until my 10:30 curfew.

"I'll hit some practice balls for you."

Tennis day was happening, and even though my loving boyfriend was being a little more stern than I had anticipated, I decided to play along. Frank began tossing tennis balls over the net, and I began missing them.

I waited for a loving and patient tennis instructor to emerge, but instead Frank said cooly, "You didn't do that right. You're holding the racquet wrong."

Holding the racquet *wrong*? This day was what was going *wrong*. I looked up, and the sun was shining warmly just like it was supposed to be, so why wasn't my boyfriend behaving like he was supposed to be? This day was going to seal our fate. We were going to live happily ever after finally finding something active we could do together. For the first time in our relationship, Frank was losing points with me. Where was my perfect boyfriend? But there was still hope. If we could actually play a set, then maybe the bonding and point earning would commence.

Holding the racquet the "right" way, the way that Frank had shown me, felt so awkward. I knew (with no help from Frank), that the object of the game was to actually hit the ball, so I switched my grip. I started walloping those fuzzy balls over the net.

"You can't hold the racquet that way! That's not the way you play tennis."

"When am I ever going to play this game except with you?"

What was going on? I thought we were playing tennis—a game that requires the player to hit the ball back over the net. Hadn't I just accomplished that? Wasn't that a good thing? Now, Frank was upset that I was hitting the ball? Didn't he want me to hit the ball? Didn't he want me to be good at this?

From the moment we had stepped onto this court something had changed—Frank. Who knew nerds could be so precise? All I wanted was to be good enough to play a game with my sweet and caring boyfriend—wherever he was.

Frank tossed up a ball and slammed it over the net. I dove and completely missed. And it was official. I was upset. What sent me over the edge was the smug look of satisfaction that flashed across my boyfriend's face. This was a side of Frank I had not seen. I could feel my frustration rising. I couldn't breathe.

"What are you trying to get me to do?" I asked the tears coming up.

"I'm trying to get you to play tennis."

Right. My tears evaporated, and I could feel my face turn bright red. The disappointment I'd felt seconds before turned into outrage. My hands rung the racquet handle like I wanted to ring Frank's neck.

I took a breath.

I didn't say anything.

Two could play that game.

I picked up an unsuspecting ball, threw it up, and pummeled it over to Frank's side of the court. He dove and missed.

"What the hell are you trying to do!?" Frank yelled from the other side of the court.

I picked up another ball and whacked it over the net. Frank again dove and missed.

"You can't hold the racquet like a baseball bat!"

"You want me to hit it or not?" I volleyed back.

This time Frank served. I ran back and backhanded the ball over. Frank couldn't get to the ball fast enough so he missed—again.

"You didn't do that right!" Frank hollered.

And with that our tennis match was done.

"I'm done playing."

"What? Why? We just started."

Frank was truly confused. I don't know if he thought our game had gone well so far or what. Maybe he was miffed he hadn't beaten me yet. Maybe he thought I'd see what a "sporty" guy he was. What I had seen was a side of Frank I never knew existed. The rules of the game had changed, and I wasn't sure how to play anymore.

"Why don't you want to play?"

If Frank truly had to ask, he really had no idea how competitive and impatient he had just been. Great. I was hurt and disappointed, and Frank didn't even have a clue as to why.

I came outside with my loving boyfriend to have fun. This outdoor guy was no fun at all. I had to stop the game before I said something I'd regret. Something tremendously intelligent like, "You suck!" Really, though, I had to stop before Frank said something that I'd really regret.

"Well, Frank, you aren't a very patient teacher," I said handing him back his racquet.

"What? What do you mean?"

"I mean, I'm done playing. I feel like it's your way or the highway here, and I'm taking the highway."

Frank was baffled. "I was just explaining the rules," he answered curtly.

"Uh huh. You're too competitive for me. I just wanted to have fun—rules or no rules."

And that was it.

I was done playing, and I was done talking. I walked off the court and waited next to the car. If Frank had been confused, he certainly understood me now.

With a single swing of the racquet, I knew a whole lot more about my boyfriend, and it wasn't just that he had cute skinny legs in his tennis shorts.

Frank will do anything to win.

Frank had unfurled his competitive macho flag and raised it sky-high. It was hard to ignore. The stern tone. The squinty, focused eyes. The impatience. I never dreamed my sweet and caring boyfriend would be pelting me with tennis balls. Even though I was well on my way to winning our first tennis match, I felt defeated.

There was no love in our tennis match. There wasn't much love in our ride home either. In the heat of the afternoon, the hot leather car seat stuck to my bare legs. I tried to focus on that sticky heat instead of my boyfriend.

Who *was* that person?

Was he always competitive?

If I were to have kids with this guy, would he go nuts when he lost at Candy Land?

I looked at Frank and tried to find that impatient competitor in this low-key guy quietly driving me home. Which one was *my* Frank?

All I could see now was that sweet gentleman who had driven an hour down here just to see me for an afternoon. I saw the guy who had stacked up heaps and heaps of loving points because he'd sent me flowers the day after he'd met me. How could that sweetheart of a boyfriend Mr. Hyde himself into such a competitive crabby-pants? In twenty minutes, Frank had lost a crazy amount of relationship points, and I wasn't sure I'd let him win them back.

Frank hadn't said two words since we got into his car. I guess he was self-aware enough to know talking to me now wasn't going to help. Maybe that was worth half a point.

After I marched to the car, he gathered our things and walked over without a word. He never tried to argue. He never tried to defend himself or condemn me. Maybe one tiny point could be awarded there.

I'm not even sure Frank realized he was behaving differently, and that knowledge might not help his case all that much. What had I done wrong except almost win? Why did Frank look at me like I was the most evil of tennis players? Didn't my legs look cute in shorts too?

Just like those other conflict-driven jocks I had dated, Frank's whole patronizing tennis-playing tone served to make me feel small. I felt like a stupid kid being scolded by an overbearing parent. Never in the entire time we'd been dating had Frank ever talked down to me like that.

But even through all the trash-talking and the arguing, my Jell-O Mind hadn't gotten the best of me. I had held my own. I had played the game until it was clear playing wasn't going to solve anything. Once I stopped playing Frank's game, Frank dropped the attitude.

Um . . . maybe I should be giving the points to myself instead of to my boyfriend.

It might not have been a perfect match (far from it), but maybe we are.

I want us to win.

I'm not a fan of my boyfriend's competitive side, but I think I can play—by not playing. I can choose to go be outdoorsy on my own or with my girlfriends, because it's clear that outdoor activities with Frank may not bring out the best in us. It doesn't take a brainiac to realize that. Frank might be as smart as he thinks he is, because apparently he realized it too—he never asked for a rematch. (Maybe he was just too afraid I'd win.)

If I can stay true to myself in the face of angry flying balls, I can handle this, because I really do want us to win at this whole relationship thing. And that's worth unlimited points. Although, I suppose it's really not about winning at all—it's how you play the game that counts.

Or in my case, how *not* to play the game.

CHAPTER 6

Will You Be Mine?

How to make Valentine's Day a romantic holiday

Chloe and Malcolm

I'm going to hire a personal shopper for my boyfriend.

We need help.

I don't think Malcolm will object to this threesome (although this probably isn't the threesome he had in mind), because he knows he needs a little help in the gift giving area of our relationship. But really I'm being selfish because I simply can't take the same unromantic tragedy befalling us again this year.

I'm trying not to panic, but the jewelry commercials have started.

On every channel, surprised girlfriends and wives are receiving tiny boxes of thoughtfulness. Each time a commercial wife squeals with glee over her little box, I am reminded of the Valentine's Day that wasn't. I'm reminded of last year's epic fail.

Finally this year I thought Malcolm and I were on the same page, but that was before he asked me the dreaded, "Any . . . ideas

. . . for . . . er . . . Valentine's Day this year?" I was wrong. We are not on the same page—we aren't even in the same novel.

This is why I figure, hiring Mal a personal shopper is the best way to go. Maybe she could use Man Language and explain to him why Valentine's Day is the Christmas of Coupledom. Then his personal shopping mistress could instruct him on what ladies like to receive on this pinkest of holidays. This way I would get to open my own little box of thoughtfulness. I'd be able to squeal—in a good way. Not like last year.

After two years of a long-distance relationship, I was so excited to finally be spending Valentine's Day with my Valentine instead of the phone! I was ready to exchange thoughtful gifts in the afternoon and lazy kisses in the evening. I couldn't wait to see what kind of glorious present Malcolm had come up with.

Malcolm had already proven himself to be a romantic with a wonderfully dumb sense of humor. In the beginning phases of our long-distance relationship, the mailbox would be fat with Mal's thoughtful homemade trinkets—nothing says "I love you" like the smell of Elmer's glue and construction paper. My clever boyfriend was a master of the handmade card with the bad pun. I could never predict what Mal would come up with next. On one of my favorites, he'd drawn a picture of tulips with a caption that read, "I've two-lips waiting for you." It doesn't get more romantic than that!

So, last year when Malcolm breezed into my apartment, said a casual, "Happy Valentine's Day," followed by the equally romantic question, "Where do you wanna eat?" I suspected this day was not going to go according to romantic plan—at least not one Malcolm had made. It was going to be a day like every other normal day consisting of takeout and *Buffy the Vampire Slayer* reruns.

I handed my boyfriend his gift, and that's when I knew. Before Mal could utter a single excuse or apology, the heavy feeling in my chest understood that he had forgotten.

Panic ran across his face. Unless he was planning on re-gifting me the ChapStick I had bought for him the day before, he was going to come up empty.

Mal mumbled apologetically, "I didn't know . . . I don't have anything . . ." He didn't need to explain. The mortified look on his face had said it all.

All my visions of dancing candy hearts vanished, and I wondered who I was dating. I couldn't believe that there was not even one piece of chocolate candy. I didn't need much—just for him to remember.

The best card Malcolm ever made for me contained a guitar pick and a small note that read, "I pick you." Malcolm should have amended that to read, "I pick you. Just not on Valentine's Day," because that's how I felt.

Short of walking my boyfriend into the nearest Walgreens and forcing him to buy me an oversized pink teddy bear, there was nothing I could do. Today would go down in the annals of our dating history—a day to tell the kids about.

"You want to know how Daddy and Mommy spent their first Valentine's Day together? Well, that's the day that Daddy forgot Mommy . . ."

It wasn't about the gift. It was never about the gift. (Maybe it was a little about the gift.) It was about the fact that I was feeling like Malcolm's insignificant other. How could my boyfriend not understand that on this day of all days, I wanted to feel special? How could he not understand me?

I had to explain it to him.

I had to tell him.

I didn't want to explain it to him.

I didn't want to tell him.

I wanted him to just know.

I feel like if I start telling Malcolm how to surprise me, it might not be as much of a surprise to me.

"Hey, Sweetie, here's the scarf you picked out for me to give to you today on this Valentine's Day."

"Oh, thank you! I've always loved scarves! How did you know?"

Where's the romance in coaching my boyfriend through romantic gift giving?

How had my boyfriend missed it all? All the stores magically turn from red and green to pink and pink the day after New Year's. The repetitiveness of the jewelry commercials alone are enough to drive a sane man crazy.

Mal looked at me with huge, sad cartoon eyes, and I knew I needed to say something.

"Just so you know," I stated calmly, "I don't need anything expensive. I just want to feel like I'm important to you."

And that was that.

Until now.

The jewelry commercials are starting—again.

'Tis the season for the shelves at Walgreens to be stacked sky-high with rows of shrink-wrapped heart-shaped boxes. 'Tis the time for Hallmark to be coated in more shades of pink than it is possible for the naked eye to detect. 'Tis the season for Malcolm to remember that he's not supposed to forget.

Over the last eleven months, I've come home to love notes on my bed and silly songs on my answering machine. Malcolm knows me better this year than last, and so clearly he will want to redeem his boyfriend honor. This year will be different.

I trust him.

"So, what do you want to do for Valentine's?"

I don't trust him.

Instead of muting the Valentine's commercials while we watch TV perhaps I should be turning them up.

"What should we do . . . for . . . er . . . this year?" Malcolm continued.

Malcolm's nervous questioning is not doing much to inspire a great deal of preplanning confidence in his Valentine's skill set.

Here I go being hurt—again. It's silly that a simple little question could smart so much, but Malcolm has opened the door wide for that familiar heavy feeling to waltz in and sit down on my chest—again. Is it wrong that I want to look at my boyfriend and tell him to just figure it out—again?

My heart can't handle another Valentine's Day Massacre. I can't do it: The disappointment. The anguish. The stale cookie eating.

Then I heard Malcolm add sheepishly, "I don't want to hurt your feelings . . . again . . ."

My boyfriend is afraid of Valentine's Day.

As a Valentine's Day honoring girlfriend, I expect a lot. A whole year passing has made it abundantly clear that my boyfriend has no idea what to expect.

Last year, Malcolm truly didn't know I had expected anything or that anything was expected of him. This year he is afraid—afraid of disappointing me. Those *subtle* questions just gave that all away. He wants to get this one exactly right. Mal is ready to spontaneously combust from all the romantic pressure. My boyfriend has a difficult time trying to choose a toothpaste at Target. Instead of a holiday to look forward too, in our world Valentine's Day is slowly becoming a holiday to fear. How is that romantic?

I could save him. I could save us. I could save myself from another year of hard Thin Mints. Instead of overwhelming my boyfriend with expectations and too many gift choices, maybe I could provide some safe parameters in which he could function.

"Why don't we have a Valentine's Day theme this year?" I suggested.

Malcolm lit up.

"Let's make this Valentine's Day pajama themed. Anything to do with PJs! What do you think?"

Malcolm was thrilled.

A personal shopper takes a person around the store and tells them what to buy, so I became more like an impersonal personal shopper. I really didn't want to take Malcolm to the mall and point out possible gift ideas, so that's how the Valentine's Day theme happened. I'm more like an *inspirational* shopper. This way Malcolm gets ideas, and I finally get my box of thoughtfulness without picking it out for him.

And isn't that what Valentine's Day is all about?

Spending it together . . .

. . . in your pajamas?

➔HUSBAND RAISING 101➔

"Can we make it through this together?"

That's what I asked myself while my husband and I were dating. If we could make it through a dating life together, we could certainly make it through a married life together. We just had to get over the dating part.

—TONILYN (who likes to refer to herself in the third person) on dating her husband

Dating your husband. The true prenuptial test. There are no easy A's, and all answers will go down on your permanent record—or on Facebook. These girlfriends needed to know how their almost-husbands would behave when conflict arose. Lily had unknowingly wounded the love of her life. Tonilyn felt *Star Wars* to be an important motivational tool. Sophie learned how to instill fear and apply fake tattoos. Chloe had the worst Valentine's Day of her dating life. Christine came face-to-face with her fiancé's stubbornness. And Ellen struggled as much with her tennis serve as with her boyfriend.

Each almost-wife chose to move past her feelings of hurt and confront the situation. Making the conscious choice to work through the conflict gave these ladies the knowledge that their boyfriends were committed to the relationship. Their fellas were in it for the long haul and wouldn't bail when the going got tough or the tough brought up *Star Wars*. This laid the groundwork for an honest and committed marriage.

SKILL BUILDING COVERED IN PART I

- ☐ How to communicate honestly and effectively
- ☐ How to truly listen to your partner during intense discussions
- ☐ How to move through feelings of blame and confusion
- ☐ How to bring up *Star Wars Episode I* in casual conversation

PART II

Can You Please Turn Down The Stereotype?

When Husbands Act Like Guys

CHAPTER 7

Role Playing

How to get your husband to move manly boxes and other girlie things

Tonilyn and Michael

I am guilty. Give me the first stone. I shall cast it—at myself. If I lived on Krypton and Superman's dad were my judge, he would sentence me to an eternity with General Zod and his cronies in that creepy two-dimensional Phantom Zone. I am *that* guilty. I'm not proud of my actions, but the first step to recovery is admitting you have a problem, right? So, here I am admitting that I have a problem: I gender profile.

"Honey, can you take out the trash?"

"Honey, would you mind changing the porch lightbulb?"

"Honey, that tree has really gone crazy. Would mind trimming it?"

Without the slightest hesitation, I ask my husband to perform tasks that have for centuries been deemed "Man of the House" chores. In my defense, these manly jobs generally involve some amount of brute strength or some sort of electrical know-how in situations where I don't know how.

It's also an established historical fact that men throughout the ages have trimmed the palace hedges and changed outdoor lightbulbs. I'm sure one of the chivalrous tasks of the Knights of the Garter was taking out the castle trash. However, I know that this is no excuse for my behavior. Just because a belief has been thus for centuries does not make it right—like bloodletting and leeches. We are no longer living in the Dark Ages. (Well, *we* are when my husband forgets to change the lightbulbs.)

My whole life, I have railed against stereotypes. I'll be the first to mumble obscenities and use obscene finger gestures if anyone tries to white-picket-fence me in. If my husband were to *expect* me to live in the kitchen in only an apron and to vacuum in nothing but a thong, I would read him his rights, use the metal handcuffs instead of the pink fuzzy ones, and haul his male ego down to the station. I want the freedom to choose who I want to be on any given day—a thong-wearing cook or a granny-panty-wearing restaurant goer. (More often I am the latter, much to the chagrin of my husband.) I don't want someone—especially the man I'm in love with—to choose who I'm supposed to be.

I am more than merely a wife, just as my husband is more than merely a husband. So I should stop putting my husband in the same kind of confining gender-specific box, right? Which reminds me . . . those boxes have been sitting in the family room way too long; he really needs to take them out to the garage and . . . Ugh! See what I mean?!

When we were first married, I wanted to share the load equally. Being equal in our marriage was extremely important to me. I wanted to pull my own weight and that included moving heavy boxes to the garage. But, ever so slowly and without thinking about it, I began asking my husband to move the boxes on his own. I began asking him to take my car in and get the oil changed—and trim the trees and replace the doors and fix the toilet.

That's about the time my husband starting hitting me with such gender profiling queries as, "What's for dinner?" and "When *you* go to the grocery store, could you get . . . ?" so he might deserve a tiny pebble thrown his way. Clearly, neither of us is completely blameless, and clearly, either of us could simply look at the other and say, "I'm not going to be that person today!" In fact, we have said that from time to time.

I'm more concerned with why I am *asking* him to be that guy. I don't want stereotypes cluttering up the house I just vacuumed.

I'm not completely sure how this household habit evolved, but I never questioned it. I never *once* questioned it, and that is what concerns me. It never occurred to me that I was stereotyping my husband, because I was simply asking him to do things that husbands are *supposed* to do. But that's like saying women are *supposed* to cook in the kitchen or *supposed* to clean the house. How is that fair? Hadn't those episodes of *Growing Pains* shown me that labels are wrong?

By continually stereotyping my husband, I wasn't seeing him for who he truly is or for who he could become—maybe he's the next Martha Stewart. I wouldn't know—he's waiting for the car at Jiffy Lube.

No more, I say! I am an equal opportunity employer! I want my husband to be and do whatever he wants to! That includes picking up a vacuum or making our bed! I want my husband to feel comfortable boiling water or cooking a hamburger! I want my Man of the House to know that he is absolutely free to be whatever he wants to be—even if that includes being the woman of the house.

CHAPTER 8

The Collector (of Messes)

How to inspire your husband to pick up his toys

Christine and Danny

Please, throw me a life preserver, because I'm drowning in stuff—piles and piles of stuff.

Stuff.

It sits in haphazard stacks on our floor, and when there's no more room on the floor, the stuff migrates. I've been tracking its migrational pattern for a bit now, and from its original place on the floor, the herd multiplies and moves to the tops of desks and the corners of unused counters. I'm not sure where it can go from here. (I pray the garage.) I can't help but wonder: Will I ever love my husband's stuff as much as I love my husband?

Danny has two great loves in his life—me and his stuff. He will not part with either. I'm happy that he's committed to sharing his life with me, but I had no idea I'd be committing to sharing my life with all his stuff too. I don't remember our intoxicated priest reciting vows like, "Do you, Christine, take Danny and all his stuff, until death do you part?" But the tipsy priest was hard to understand what with all the slurring. Who knows what I really agreed to?

My husband is a collector of DVDs, CDs, baseball cards, and action figures. Over thirty-five years of carefully preserved collectibles share our home and tell the story of Danny's life. (I've never collected anything for an entire lifetime—except maybe wrinkles.) It must be comforting for him to look around the house and see his life go by in stacks. Danny can instantly remember what girl he was dating in 1984 just by looking at the Peter Venkman action figure in the *Ghostbusters* stack sitting next to his Salieri figure from *Amadeus*.

To Danny his collectible stacks are sacred, and these piles shall never be moved or touched. To my untrained eye, Danny's stuff simply looks like stacks and stacks and piles and piles of clutter—uncleanable clutter that's suffocating me.

Walking to the kitchen at 2 a.m. for something as simple as a glass of water becomes a terrifying task. In the dark, I can only make out tall, scary shadows that change shape as I tiptoe past. Not too mention, said toes are in constant peril; for at any moment I may whack them on a stack of carefully preserved baseball card albums or stub them on a box of action figures.

I feel like I'm a character in a horror movie creeping through my pitch-black living room. Any minute now my phone will ring and I'll hear, "What's *your* favorite scary movie?" Strangely, the voice won't sound like the altered voice from *Scream*, it'll sound like a giant Donald Duck plush toy. My house is scaring me.

Even though I may not be able to see my walls for all the stacking, I can see that I'm not feeling comfortable in my own home. These stacks of "collectibles" have no practical purpose except to clutter. Danny's stuff doesn't help me clean the floor or cut a pizza. It just sits there. Its only purpose—to take up vast amounts of space.

I want to come home to an organized space where I feel safe and cozy. The world outside can be crazy and unnerving—all those crazy drivers and strange people twirling pointy "APARTMENT FOR RENT" signs in my face overwhelm me. There's so much chaos in the outside world—may I please have some order in my personal, private, inside one?

"Danny, could we move some of this stuff to the garage? I'm feeling a little suffocated . . ."

"*No!* It's not temperature regulated in the garage."

That would have been too easy.

In order to appeal to my more organized tastes, Danny has tried to reassure me time and again that his collections are, in fact, not clutter. The mountains of plastic figures, books, and baseball cards that assault my senses are, according to Danny, organized. For instance, his CDs are organized according to genre, artist, album, and release date. A person won't find Tom Waits' new CD next to the *Waterworld* soundtrack, and the Bee Gees would never ever be lazily placed next to *The Best Little Whorehouse in Texas* cast recording. (Oh, wait. That last one is mine.) This new piece of knowledge has not made it possible for me to breathe any easier or made his stuff magically move to the garage.

"What if we put some of your stuff in boxes to keep it safe," he was listening, "—and then moved it into the garage?"

He shook his head.

That would have been too easy.

Danny's stuff is as much a part of him as his arms or his uvula. I don't think I will ever be able to separate him from it. And I can't be completely sure, but I think Danny is trying to convert me. His plan is simple. Keep his collections in my sights, and perhaps I will grow to enjoy them as much as he does. He's definitely trying to encourage my love for his stuff. This possibly stems from the real fear that he might come home to find I've listed all of his goods on e-Bay and retired to the Caribbean.

Everywhere I look I see bits of Danny in clutter form. I'd like to see bits of carpet and counter space. Or I'd like to see bits of me. Seeing more of me in my house would entail seeing more negative space in my house—which would actually be a positive. Maybe then I can come home to a safe place and kick off my shoes and relax.

Danny has offered no solution to removing or organizing his colossal amounts of stuff except that he wants his stuff to remain where it is. But I'm having nightmares about a giant Elmer Fudd figure attacking me and forcing me to hunt "wabbits."

"Danny, what if we went and bought some great shelves so that you could display all of your stuff in your office?"

"Sure."

That was too easy.

Danny loves his stuff. I love Danny, but not as much as he loves his stuff. I do love his stuff more now that it is properly categorized and sitting pretty on bookshelves.

His DVDs, CDs, baseball cards, action figures, and plush toys all look beautifully organized living in their places atop their assigned shelves. No more mass migrations and no more clutter. At last, I can feel safe. At last I can breathe.

"Christine, Honey—my mom just called. She wants me to come home and get my stuff. It's cluttering up their attic."

I think we're going to need some bigger shelves.

CHAPTER 9

The Second Coming

How to deal with a threesome—you, your husband, and your mother-in-law

Ellen and Frank

"Why won't you say something?" I asked through heavy sobs.

"She doesn't mean it that way," he answered with a shrug.

"So, you would rather upset me, your wife, than upset your mother?"

"I guess so."

And that would be the end of it. Every Sunday our conversation was the same. Every Sunday for eight months now, not one word had altered. Each dramatic conversation with my husband left me feeling more alone than the last. Each conversation left me more angry than the last. I felt like I was stuck in some cheesy, horribly scripted Lifetime drama where the heroine was always crying.

I should change the channel. I should change the channel, stop crying, and tune in to a sensible Discovery Channel program.

But I'm too sucked in. Curled up in front of the TV, box of Kleenex on my lap, I wonder if my plucky Lifetime heroine-of-the-week will ever overcome her obstacles and win. I want to know how she does it, because clearly in my life, I am incapable. I need Valerie Bertinelli or Meredith Baxter (Birney) to leap through my television set and tell me what to do. Their characters have been through it all—seemingly insurmountable obstacles—and yet, somehow they've prevailed. One thing is certain: I know my obstacle. My obstacle even has a name: Liz. My obstacle happens to be my mother-in-law.

My father-in-law had taken a job that kept him out of town, so it fell to my husband, Frank, to complete all the "boy jobs" around his childhood home. So, while Frank mowed the lawn and dealt with all things green, my mother-in-law Liz fixed all of us dinner. From the outside, and certainly from Frank's front-yard perspective, this seemed like it should be a lovely evening spent bonding and laughing. But the truth is, Liz really liked to use this time to hover over our nine-month-old daughter and criticize me.

Like a pistol shot signaling the start of a race, the lawn mower motor whirring outside signaled the start of Liz's inquisition regarding my parenting skills: "Where did you get that outfit for Jenny? How much did you spend? Why is she wearing it? What laundry detergent are you using? How much is she sleeping? How much are you feeding her?"

After the first barrage of crazy questions was completed, an acerbic observation or two invariably followed. "Ellen, that outfit seems to be too tight for her," or how about, "You don't take Jenny outside enough. Babies need fresh air. You should really take her outside more." I answered her questions as politely as I could, hoping that Frank's bathroom break would distract Liz long enough for me to recite my mantra: "She doesn't mean to be that way. She doesn't mean to be that way," over and over and over again. Maybe if I said it enough, I would believe it.

The inquisition didn't end until the homemade dessert had been devoured and the after-dinner coffee consumed. For six hours, I fielded all manner of questions and comments laced with mistrust and judgment. I tried to ignore the negative undercurrent and bury my frustration as best I could. It wasn't my place to say anything. She was my husband's mother, and I didn't want to cause problems by talking back.

Growing up, I was never allowed to talk back to any adult, even if they deserved it. My parents had instilled this tenet early on, and it was so much a part of me that the mere thought of hurling back a snide remark at an elder made my entire body freeze. I became a frozen, smiling statue, incapable of speech. The only thing that didn't freeze was the angry, spinning knot in my stomach.

Since I spent most of my Sunday evenings in this smiley-frozen state, I had hoped that Frank would talk to his mother for me. Frank was my husband, after all, and that's what husbands do—stand up for their wives. Right?

Here's where my Lifetime drama would get even better. (Jennifer Love Hewitt had nothing on me, because, to my shock and confusion, yet another obstacle was to be hurled at the feet of our already downtrodden heroine. Get your Kleenex boxes ready—to throw.) When I finally bluntly explained to Frank how his mother had been treating me in his absence, I expected my loving husband to be horrified and immediately leap to my rescue. There wasn't even a tiny hop. "Just ignore her," was Frank's lame response. He didn't seemed bothered in the slightest.

That hurt. The phrase "dagger through the heart" doesn't even begin to cover it. My broken heart believed, above all things, that marriage was a partnership where each person had the other's back. Frank and I were supposed to be a team. But when it came to his mother, I was totally left holding the ball. Why wouldn't my husband defend me? Why wouldn't my husband stand up to his mother for me? Deep down, I became afraid that Frank didn't love me enough to stand up for me. I was afraid that his wife and daughter would always come last, and that's really what caused the perpetual waterworks in the car each Sunday. Yes, Liz's behavior hurt and I didn't feel like I deserved it, but what hurt more was my husband's inaction. That's what made me feel completely alone. And what could I do about it?

I had truly expected Frank to step into his new role as husband and father easily. It's true that Frank and I were basically newlyweds with a newborn. Being married less than two years and then having a baby change a person's life quickly. Sure, he had been a son longer than he had been a husband, but at some point being the partner of your partner comes first, and being the child of your parent comes second, right? Frank had missed the tutorial. His childhood habit of placating his mother was not having the same calming effect on his wife. Not even close.

Another Sunday came and went, and again through tears, I tried to persuade my husband to become a team player and say something to his mother. "Frank, why won't you stand up for me?" and then I added quietly, "I think I'm a good mom."

"That's just the way she is. She's been that way my whole life. Just ignore her," was his solution.

Still not what I wanted to hear. That's when the usual Sunday conversation with my husband took an unexpected turn. My percolating anger somehow found its way up from my chest, and I heard myself clearly warning, "One of these times, Frank, I'm going to lose my temper."

I didn't know what to do. What I wanted more than anything was help from the man I loved, but Frank seemed so nonplussed. I wished I could have been so lax about the the whole thing, but each time I was berated by his mother, I felt betrayed by my husband. That feeling of complete and utter betrayal tightened that familiar angry knot in my stomach.

Maybe I could just avoid Sundays all together. I put this idea to Frank, but then he ever-so-practically pointed out our financial situation. That one Sunday dinner helped out our weekly budget so much that we literally couldn't afford to say no. I was completely stuck. That's when I began daydreaming of standing up to my mother-in-law. If I couldn't stand up to her in real life, I could stand up to her in my dreams.

In my dreams, I was good. I came up with the best comebacks ever! They were quick and laced with just enough bite to get her attention, but subtle enough that I still looked like the good guy. I wanted to be that plucky heroine who conquered all. I imagined that every Lifetime movie heroine who ever tackled a drama was giving me a pat on the back and welcoming me into their ranks of True Plucky Heroine of the week. I wanted to leave my Kleenex box in the bathroom, hear the closing music swell, and see the end credits roll.

Again, the following Sunday, I found myself at Liz's house. As the lawn mower whirred, I braced myself for the volley of questions that would undoubtedly be unleashed. And thus it began . . .

"What happened to those outfits Jenny was wearing the other week? The cute one with the dog on the front?" Liz inquired.

With that almost polite inquiry, I thought that perhaps this Sunday I might escape the usual criticisms. In an attempt to have a casual conversation I offered, "I've got a good friend who just had a little girl, so I gave the clothes to her."

Liz turned to face me, her features suddenly drawn and tight. Her brown eyes grew wide with anger and disbelief. She stood stock-still.

"I cannot believe that you took money from *my son* and gave it to a girlfriend of yours!" she exploded.

I'd been ambushed. I felt the wave of shock overtake me. I was a frozen, smiling statue. My feet were glued to the oriental rug below, my brain went foggy, and even though I felt my mouth fall open, nothing audible escaped my lips. Yet another Sunday, I was a deer trapped in the headlights of Liz's rage.

My mother-in-law glared at me—waiting. In my shock, I realized that Liz was waiting for me to actually respond. I managed to get the feeling back in my mouth and stammered, "Well . . . um. . . . right. . . Jenny outgrew them, and my, uh, friend has less money than we do to buy clothes . . . so I gave them to her. . . ."

Liz was less than pleased.

"YOU DO NOT TAKE MONEY FROM *MY SON* AND THROW IT AWAY!" she railed.

I could feel the anger in my stomach beginning its frenzied spinning, and I let it. I was scared to death to stand up to my husband's mother. I wanted to swallow my anger, to be that sweet girl I had been brought up to be, but I just couldn't take another moment of this. I had done nothing to deserve Liz's wrath except marry her son, and it finally hit me—Frank wasn't going to stand up for me. If he wasn't, then it was about time I did! By giving myself that permission, I broke free. I could feel the hot, angry words forming in the back of my throat. I surrendered to the heat. Farrah Fawcett had nothing on me.

"WHO GIVES YOU THE RIGHT TO PLAY GOD?! NO ONE JUDGES ME BUT GOD!" I screamed, letting months of hurt and betrayal fly free.

I could feel the tears coming, but I'd be damned if I let that woman see me cry. I scooped up my daughter, marched into my husband's childhood room, shut the door, and locked it.

When Frank came in to the aftermath of my row with Liz, he was shocked—shocked that his seemingly sweet wife had stood up for herself in such a loud way. There was no mistaking it—that day, I had clearly found my grown-up voice. Patty Duke would have been so proud.

And my own private heroic moment was to have an unexpected side effect. Finding my voice proved to be the catalyst for my husband to find his. That very same day Frank had that long-awaited talk with his mother. I don't know what was said, but from that moment on, my relationship with Liz changed too. Her criticisms stopped (mostly), and she began to adopt a quieter tone. Whatever Frank said worked. She was trying to accept me as her son's chosen wife and the capable mother of her grandchildren. I'd take it.

My Kleenex box now sits prettily on my bathroom counter. I don't need it much for my TV-watching or for my life. I can move more easily past channel 145 now, safe in the knowledge that I am the plucky heroine I always wanted to be. That Sunday, the quiet child in me found her very powerful and very loud adult voice, and that Sunday also forever changed my relationship with my husband. That Sunday, we became a team. I learned that playing on a team also means that one player may have to hold the ball just a little longer, until the other player is ready to take that final step toward the winning touchdown. Cheesy line, but true. Lifetime, Television for Women, if you're reading this, feel free to use it.

CHAPTER 10

Doing It Yourself

How to clean and organize your husband

Lily and Gus

It's my problem. I could do a little research in the matter. Perhaps go to the bookstore (I think they still have those) and pick up a few books. I fear, however, that this course of action will be of no help, because the true essence of the problem lies here at home. The problem is lying all over the dining room table. The problem is lying on the hardwood floor. The problem is my husband doesn't notice.

I'd like to see life from my husband's point of view. What a wonderful world it must be! Gus' world is free of pesky things like dust and mildew. It is a world of perpetually Pledged countertops and hardwood floors as reflective as patent leather shoes.

His is a magical world where doughnuts appear on the kitchen counter every morning. *Poof!* (Oh, whoops, that last one is from my magical world.) In Gus' world little things like grime, muck, and last year's stacked Christmas presents do not exist. To quote the brilliant and well-spoken Tina Fey, "I want to go to there."

If only I lived in Gus' world, I wouldn't care a whit about this cleaning charade. Hold that thought! Maybe that's the key—to try and see our house from his perspective! What a wild idea! There would be no more inner steaming. There would be no more annoyed wishing that Gus would clean up. I could learn to appreciate the disorganization!

If I saw our house like my husband does, I wouldn't notice all the little pieces of food stuck to the kitchen counter. I wouldn't see a lone man-sized gardening glove waiting listlessly on the front stoop for over a month. What must that be like? To walk through the house and not recognize the stack of mail and useless opened envelopes piled unevenly on our dining room table?! (Those piles never diminish in size either. Every morning they multiply like breeding rabbits or gremlins who've been fed after midnight. It's eerie.)

Wouldn't it be *loverly* never to feel the overpowering urge to throw away old mail and newspapers? I could learn to revel in our ever-growing grass! The kids playing *Children of the Corn* in our front yard sure have.

I can change! I can fight my instincts. I don't have to be who I am! I can learn to live in a less organized world! Easy!

I'm afraid.

I'm scared that if I learn to see our house from Gus' point of view, I might drown in leftover kitchen counter sandwich crumbs and mounds of men's unhung trousers never to be heard from again. Rescue crews might find me a week later barely alive . . .

"How did you survive that horrible ordeal?"

"Well, I was able to eat sandwich crumbs for sustenance, and I sang show tunes about cleaning in my head."

Or even more unnerving, maybe I would end up on a TLC reality show. I'd suddenly be thrust onto a nightmare of a show centering around people who can't seem to throw away any printed paper product.

These reality show guests would agree to talk to therapists about their overpowering need to hold on to used bills and newspapers. Its title—*Paper Pushers*. The guests would tearily admit to pushing the paper around on their desks or dining room tables so it looks like they are, in fact, cleaning. But really it's like a child pushing around his vegetables to prove to his parents he ate his abhorrent brussels sprouts. Oh, the horror. *Paper Pushers*. Not a bad idea actually. I should call TLC.

I suppose I shouldn't be so hard on my husband. Really, he's a great guy. This is why I married him. And I'm not as perfect as I think I am. I must engage in horrible habits that irritate him too. Extremely annoying habits like cleaning up after myself and straightening my side of the bathroom.

My husband has what might be considered a more casual approach to cleaning. His laid-back approach generally consists of not getting it done. I'm sure my husband would disagree. For example, take Gus' Christmas presents from last year. They were put away—this Christmas.

At this point I know better than to ask him to clean up. I used to ask him to pick up his mail from 2001 off of the dining room table. But what happened next I will always find strange: Not only was my polite suggestion misconstrued as nagging, but the cleaning project was not completed. I'm not trying to be a nag, I'm simply trying to walk through the dining room.

Gus isn't trying to be mean. That is I hope he's not sneaking into the kitchen under the cover of night to sprinkle bread crumbs on the counter only to irritate me. I'm assuming he's not stacking papers in the dining room with a maniacal laugh. I doubt he's leaving out that solitary gardening glove only to vex me. (How very Jane Austin of him.) He's simply not bothered by any mess. He's being who he is.

I am bothered by the mess. I am being who I am. It must be my issue.

In remaining true to my tidy self and my get-it-done-now-instead-of-later attitude, I decided to get it done now. I thought I'd be helpful and clean up my husband's mail, and his unhung pants, and his kitchen mess.

Our cleaning pattern had been, I wait as long as I can before I clean. (I suppose that's really *my* cleaning pattern.) There's only so long I can tolerate piles of pants and clumps of toothpaste on the bathroom counter.

So there I was happily wiping down counters, throwing things in the trash, and hanging up pants when I was met with a sour and disappointed husband. He looked at me like I had just eaten his last doughnut (okay, maybe I had) and said quietly, "I was going to do that."

I was stunned. Mostly, because he really believed what he said. I felt like I'd been caught cleaning behind his back. I'd think a lot of husbands would be thrilled. "Honey, you cleaned the house?! Why thank you! Let me buy you a dozen doughnuts!" Not my husband. Maybe he just felt guilty, but I'm sensing it's more than that. I'm just not so sure what. Which brings me back to my initial query: Is this my issue? Maybe I wasn't giving him enough time.

I could try adjusting my inner cleaning clock to Gus Time. Gus Standard Time always runs slower than Lily Standard Time. Gus will eventually (mostly) clean up his stuff.

Maybe I'm just too fast for him. Maybe my go-getter attitude is a little too go and get. Maybe falling back instead of springing forward is the way to do it. I could learn to take more time for myself and less time rewashing the dishes. I could learn to relax and put my feet up—on top of a stack of last year's newspapers. I could do this. I could let Gus mow the lawn.

The lawn. Like some, I am not afraid of the lawn. I am not overwhelmed by its size and shape. I look at the lawn, and I see an opportunity. I welcome this chance to make some organized beauty happen. I'm delighted to water our lawn. I don't mind cutting our grass. The sound of the mower lulls me into an organized-feeling coma.

As the man in this house, Gus feels like it's his chore to water and mow. The problem is he doesn't always hear his call of duty before the lawn turns a dehydrated brown or is as tall as an elephant's eye.

Gus said he would mow the grass, so I will take him at his word. I can wait. No matter that the yard is already an ocher shade and tickling my ankles. I can wait. I can do this. I can slow down my cleaning clock to give my husband the time he needs to feel like a man. Perhaps he just hasn't known the deep satisfaction of completing a chore? I will give that joy to my husband. I will let him have that lovely feeling. Who am I to take away that feeling of efficient bliss?

I am a woman who had waited two weeks and was staring blankly at a tall but dying burnt sienna lawn. I might not be able to save myself from myself, but I could definitely save my lawn from my husband.

Gus arrived home to a freshly cut and watered lawn.

With sad puppy-dog eyes and an emasculated sting to his voice, he said, "I was going to do that."

I heard it that time. How many times had I listened to this mumbled phrase after picking up after him? How many times had I been irked? How may times had I been confused? This time I *heard* it—the shame. I could see myself and our house through Gus' eyes: I was a tidy whirlwind of a woman with whom Gus just couldn't keep up. He had tried. He just couldn't.

Gently, I explained to my husband what kind of a girl he married. I was not a dirty girl. I felt more comfortable doing things now instead of later. I felt better in a house that was structured and together—everything in its place.

I explained to Gus that this desire had absolutely nothing to do with him and everything to do with me. My go-getter chore attitude would never be a reflection on his lack of chore doing—like he might have felt. This was just an extension of who I was. Who I am. I just like to get it done, and I'll do it myself if I have to.

I could see the confusion abate and the tension leave his forehead.

I am clean. My husband is not. This is who we are, and we know that now. We can see that. Now, I can walk around and clean to my heart's content. Gus understands. Well, mostly he understands. I've learned to leave the papers on the dining room table for Gus to handle (sometime in 2021), and the lawn still remains a source of confusion. But I've stopped getting annoyed. Well, I've stopped getting *as* annoyed.

Gus now understands that I'm a neatnik—well, he understands more. He knows that I just get it done and it's nothing personal. I'm not angrily cleaning the house to get back at him for not cleaning the house. I've noticed that lately Gus has taken to cleaning the kitchen counters without my even mentioning it. The well-meaning sponge strokes sparkling in the sunlight are a dead giveaway. Maybe he's finally feeling that lovely chore-doing sense of accomplishment. A clean girl can dream.

I've also learned a little secret. Asking Gus sharply to "clean up" never worked. If I rephrase my query with softer words such as, "Gus would you *help me* clean up?" my delightful husband will ask me where the vacuum cleaner is and join me in tidying. Who knew such a simple turn of phrase could be so helpful? I'm guessing it has something to do with my husband wanting to help me vs. feeling like he must put away his playthings. Who really *likes* to put away their things? Well, me.

Please don't tell him that I rewipe the kitchen counters late at night while he's asleep.

CHAPTER 11

The One Thing Boys Want

How to bring more romance into your marriage

Tonilyn and Michael

"You don't have sex with me enough."

My husband hands me a clean plate and that piece of sexy information.

"I have sex with you more than anyone else."

It's true. I do have sex with my husband more than anyone else. But Michael took no solace in my uproarious jape. I distinctly saw a scowl curl his lip. He can't be serious.

"You don't have sex with me enough" becomes an instant challenge. I rip the next clean plate out of his hand and hurl it to the floor. The plate breaks into a million pieces as we drop down on the hard linoleum tile and go for it!

Not so much.

That's not going to happen.

First of all, I'd never break my Official Daffy Duck Collector Plate, and in this moment I'm slightly more confused than hot for my husband. We have enough sex.

Maybe this was just my husband's attempt at a romantic kitchen seduction. Was his casual observation only meant to open the door for a new kind of culinary romance? Was it a new chapter in Michael's handbook of *The Art of Husbandly Seduction*? I like new chapters.

So I waited for a playful smirk and a loving gesture that would signify the start of our soon-to-be private time. What better way to dismiss my husband's would-be-criticism than to have all of the sex right now?

I stood in the kitchen prepared to be seduced. I said nothing. I wanted the moment to remain unspoiled. I waited to accept my husband's amorous advances. I looked forward to hearing him whisper how much he loved me—how happy he was we were together. This was my favorite part—the seduction. The romance. I can't imagine I'll ever outgrow hearing my husband's tender words sighed against the nape of my neck.

Unless my husband's new seduction technique consisted of methodically handing me clean spoons in an expectant silence, there was to be no seducing. He was totally serious. Time to readjust.

"What do you mean?" I asked, trying to keep it light.

"I mean, you don't have sex with me enough."

Ah. Now, I understand. *What?!*

I never thought we'd be one of those couples. Those couples who you see on TV talk shows discussing their sex life with as much as passion as if they were talking about assembling a dishwasher. I thought that being married was when true Sexy Time began.

Once the man of my dreams married me, I would always know that I was loved and treasured and cherished. I would forever feel a close bond because I was married. Well, where's all the romance? Where's all the sex? Apparently, it's just on reruns of *Sex and the City* and episodes of *True Blood*.

I was now officially confused. I could detect no tone. I've gotten pretty adept at identifying different husband tones, and I could uncover no anger, malice, or frustration hidden beneath his words. This sentence was decidedly tone-free. His statement sounded more matter-of-fact—like a casual afterthought. More along the lines of, "Honey, we're out of sugar, and oh yeah, you don't have sex with me enough."

Now, I'm not sure how to respond. I'm not sure if I'm supposed to respond. It's possible this is more of a rhetorical statement. Maybe Michael is just stating a preference, like, "You don't buy enough strawberry ice cream." That would be an easy fix. I'd just go to the store and get him more of the strawberry ice cream. I'm not sure I can just get him more of the sex. I blame the nuns.

My high school years were spent in an all-girls Catholic high school. The "best years of my life," when I should've been having fun making out with cute boys at football games, were spent studying morality and memorizing the Seven Mortal Sins that would send me to straight to hell. (Making out with cute boys at football games was one of them.)

Senior year my entire class was subjected to a religion course on Marriage and Family Life taught by aging Catholic Sisters, aka *nuns*. These are pious women who have never been married. These are saintly souls who have presumably never had sex. I'm not sure if they were the best candidates for educating young girls about the expectations of marriage and family life.

I was bombarded with fear propaganda. Phrases such as "Pet your dog, not your date" rang in my ears, and one all-important message was repeated over and over—"Be careful, boys only want *one thing*." I was savvy enough at seventeen to know this "one thing" was not that elusive vinyl-caped Jawa *Star Wars* action figure.

The phrase "Boys only want one thing" buried itself deep in my psyche. The possibility that boys *only* wanted sex from us girls scared me. I saw my girlfriends give it up, and then I saw their boys break it up.

My girlfriends were heartbroken, and it was painful to watch. There were probably other reasons for their breakups, but in my teenaged world it seemed like these high school boys had gotten what they wanted and moved on. I decided I would never give it up so easily. I guess I still don't.

The only noise in the kitchen was the rattling of the silverware being put away. Michael was silent. He was waiting for me to respond.

"We just did last week . . .," I scrambled.

"It was a month ago."

That is totally untrue.

"It hasn't been a month . . .," I countered with a you-can't-be-serious laugh.

"Tonilyn, it was a month ago."

He could be serious.

And he was.

Michael looked at me with such abject disappointment that I instantly wanted to fix it. For a moment, I considered trying to find my inner vixen. Pulling him aggressively down onto the kitchen tile for Sexy Time was a surefire way to make him feel better—and prove him wrong.

But my inner vixen is more of a timid mouse who likes to read Charlotte Brontë novels and color quietly in the corner. This particular Afternoon Delight might have made Michael feel a whole lot better, but I knew I'd just feel weird. It would have felt forced, and I can't operate like that. I don't turn on like a switch.

It has occurred to me that my husband might be happier if I had an On and Off Sex Switch installed. I'd imagine it's similar to a V-chip, just the exact opposite. It'd be so much easier for him. This way he could just turn me "on" whenever he wanted without actually *turning me on*. With this magical switch Michael wouldn't have to put in any of the oh-so-draining emotional work it takes to work me up. He wouldn't have to talk to me or cuddle with me or work that arduous *ten whole minutes* on seducing me. (How depleting.)

I've heard it said that "sex can just be sex." It can just be a fun physical act between two consenting people. I get it—for them. I've never gotten it for me.

Late at night when I'm flipping channels between Time Life music infomercials, I've found myself seduced by the sheer craziness of those Girls Gone Wild. I've wondered what it would be like to be one those girls—they look like they are having so much fun with all that crazy sex!

Those girls are having such a wildly good time with all the sex and sexiness that I wonder what it must be like not to care. (Copious amounts of alcohol probably help.) I wonder what it's like not to need the sweet words and the romance. I wonder if I can do it. But I know I can't. I've already gone that route—it was called my twenties.

Whether it's the Catholic Sisters who corrupted me or just my own personal desire, I want my sex to have meaning. I want *more meaning* while my husband simply wants *more*.

I will concede that a month is a long time for us to go without, so I understand why my husband is stating that there has not been enough. The truth is, I could just as easily state that there is not enough romance. This would directly contribute to his lack of enough sex. As a married adult, I still want to feel valued and special. My husband is caring and generous, but his sex drive only has two modes—on or off. I'm still trying to figure out the off mode.

With the last fork put away, my husband's sex-starved puppy-dog eyes stare listlessly at me. The weight behind those baby blues serves to bring my wifely guilt right up from my chest to the back of my throat. I know from his point of view this sexual crisis could be quickly averted. Have more sex. Easy. The problem is I am not.

"What would you like to do about it?" I asked, trying to find a solution.

"I'd like for you to have more sex with me."

Ah. I knew the solution would be simple. If only I'd thought of that.

"You know, I'd like to have more sex too"—which was true. "I just need a little more romance to get me in the mood"—which was also true.

"You know, sex can just be sex."

Ah, that's where I'd heard that phrase before. How do I explain to my husband that my insides have a really hard time digesting the whole concept of "sex can be just sex"?

"My insides have a really hard time digesting the whole concept of 'sex can be just sex.'"

Michael gave me what I'd like to term a "yeah, right" kind of look. This information clearly did not compute. I understand that boys don't get it. They probably don't get it because they don't need it. Maybe not all women need a sweet-talkin', but this one does.

A successful marriage is built on compromise, but I'm just not sure I can compromise on this particular issue. I'd feel like I was compromising myself. Michael and I are not living in the thirteenth century. It's not the Middle Ages where I'm forced to bed my husband whenever and if ever he should so desire. (Although I wouldn't mind a brocade gown or two.)

I stared at Michael trying to figure out a way to fix this for both us.

"I wish I could just drop down on the tile and go for it, but I can't. I wish I could be that for you, but I can't. I need the love first." Then stealing a line from *Jerry Maguire* I added, "That's just how I'm built."

The first half of that sentence made Michael's eyes light up like they do when he sees a cupcake. But the spark faded swiftly and the expression that now occupied his face was hard to read. I couldn't give in here. I wasn't trying to be stubborn. I wasn't trying to be a withholding wench or a tease. I wasn't trying to barter sex for love. I was trying to be true to myself.

I stood in the kitchen looking up at my husband hoping he understood everything I was saying—hoping he understood *me*. My husband was just going to have to expend the mental and physical energy it took to seduce me. My husband was just going to have to take that whole ten minutes and win me over. I need the warmth and the tenderness. That's just how it has to be.

"I love you," my husband whispered.

Ah, see. It doesn't even take ten minutes.

CHAPTER 12

A Brief History

How to show your husband what the washer and dryer are for

Ellen and Frank

There they are again.

Whoosh. Flop.

I try to focus on something else.

Whoosh. Flop.

Whoosh. Flop.

Maybe I can pair socks up in my head as they fly past.

Whoosh. Flop.

This lasts one spin cycle before I spot the renegade underwear whooshing and flopping around inside the dryer. Even if I turn my head to look at all the other washers and dryers lined up neatly against the wall, the happy orange stripe on the waistband in front of me gets my attention every time. I'm obsessed with my husband's underwear.

Whoosh. Flop.

I can't watch anymore. I close my eyes hoping to see organized darkness, but what I end up seeing are piles and piles and piles of dirty underwear—well, one pile really. I can't escape Frank's underwear—here or at home. My husband's unclean untidy-whitey pile in the bathroom corner is driving me nuts.

Frank and I are new to this whole being married thing, so I started picking up his underwear as a loving wifely gesture. Really though, I just can't stand to look at them. I assumed that Frank would offer to help or at least offer a thank-you.

He never offered one word.

It's like he believes that some sort of Underwear Fairy sneaks into our apartment and washes and folds his dirty delicates. Or maybe he thinks his mom sneaks in and does it for him. More than likely, he doesn't think about it at all—which is what hurts the most.

How hard is it to pick up your underwear and put it in the dirty clothes bin? Was my husband raised in a fluff and fold? Well, as it turns out—sort of.

On laundry day at Frank's house, his dirty items disappeared from their home on the floor and magically reappeared clean and folded on his bed. I'm not sure Frank would even recognize a washer in a household appliance lineup. He might mistake it for a dishwasher or a tiny cat Jacuzzi.

I prefer not to have his unclean untidy-whities pile up in the bathroom, so I gather up his underwear for him every morning. (Truth be told, I'd much rather be a part of a morning jewelry gathering ritual. Instead of picking up a pair of discarded underwear, I'd pick up a pretty necklace.)

Whoosh. Flop.

Now the sound of my husband's underwear tumbling in the dryer aggravates me to no end. I'm tired of cleaning up after Frank.

Last time I checked, our shared space is exactly that—shared. I want to feel comfortable in the space I *share* with my husband. Most of all, I want to feel like my husband cares. Our conversations as of late haven't made me all that confident on that point.

When I ask him to put his underwear in the dirty clothes hamper, he only ever asks, "Why?" Even trying to explain how we're sharing a small space and how doing this one thing would really help me out makes no difference. I thought I had married a helpful man. As it turns out, I married a man who likes having his own personal laundress.

The daily laundry pickup is annoying, but not as annoying as my husband not caring about how I feel about it. Never once has he offered to do the laundry. I don't want to spend the rest of my marriage washing clothes and cleaning up my husband's underwear. I thought we were supposed to be a team?

Whoosh. Flop. Ka-Chunk.

The dryer stopped.

Huh.

Maybe I should too.

Ignoring Frank's underwear would be tough. I'd tried this solution before and succeeded—for a total of six hours. The orderly part of me couldn't stand it. It was so hard to walk in the bathroom and see that ugly pile taking up what tiny personal space I had. I had to get rid of them. Piles of underwear are very distracting when one is trying to take a relaxing bath.

If I did truly stop cleaning up after my husband, I'd really have to commit. There would be no other way around it. The only other possibility would be to leave all of his underwear in the dryer and tell him that the dryer ate them. But that wouldn't work. He'd just buy more. I can't control my husband's underwear pile.

I bade the dryer a fond farewell and wondered what the coming week would hold.

Monday the floor held a lonely pair of Frank's underwear, as it usually did. I suppose I wasn't too surprised by this development.

Tuesday and Wednesday the pile multiplied at its usual speed and started spreading out from the corner into the center of the bathroom. I stared at it for a while hoping I could use my mental power to banish the image from my mind, but so far this technique hadn't worked. I needed more practice. I thought, "I bet I can try tomorrow."

Thursday afternoon, I peeked into Frank's underwear drawer just to make sure my count was right. Three more days. Three more days of clean underwear. He'd better start rationing.

Finally, when I thought the pile might sprout a mouth and start laughing at me, the fateful morning arrived.

Frank opened up his underwear drawer to find it completely empty.

"Honey, where's all my clean underwear?"

"Wow honey, I don't know," I called from the bathroom.

"But I saw you do laundry the other day. Where's all my stuff?" He asked now standing in the bathroom door.

"Well, I did everything in the hamper . . ."

"I don't understand it," he pondered while he unconsciously shuffled the pile with his feet. "Where did all my underwear go?"

"Honey . . . look down . . ."

That day Frank went to work "commando" style.

Frank is now on board with the whole laundry thing, because now my husband is able to find that elusive laundry hamper on a daily basis. Frank's underwear no longer lives on the bathroom floor, and I finally live in an organized apartment.

I guess going to work underwear-free wasn't as sexy and comfortable as he might have thought—all that whooshing and flopping.

CHAPTER 13

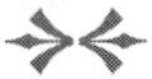

Playing the Game

How to achieve a high score in your gamer's life

Chloe and Malcolm

It's not a pretty thing, but I am jealous. This jealousy drives me to think sneaky thoughts and concoct dark, desperate scenarios. I don't want this ugly feeling to force me into a life of crime causing me to spend the rest of my days worrying if my villainous black cape is wrinkle-free. That's not me. I have to find a better way of dealing with this.

It's unfortunate that my rational self has become quite adept at rationalizing, because in this particular context, I believe jealousy is not only appropriate, it's acceptable. It's a perfectly normal wifely reaction when you know deep down that your husband is interested in another. My simmering jealousy just shows how much I care, how much I love him.

Malcolm is constantly reassuring me that I'm his only love—that he loves me above all others. But I know that's not right. If that were true, he wouldn't be off playing with his mistress. What hurts more is there's a life that lives within me that Mal's *other* can never possess. I know this because I am actually *alive*. I can't understand why my husband loves spending more time with his computer than with me. I need answers. I'd Google it, but he's on the computer.

I can't compete. Hugs and kisses from his wife are no match for the magic spell Malcolm's computer can conjure for him.

Mal loves his video games. When he walks through our front door, he'll choose playing on the computer over talking with me. I know this because when he walks through our front door he chooses playing on the computer over talking to me. Short of donning skimpy outfits like a Mage in *World of Warcraft*, I'm not sure what I can do to get his attention. I just don't think I have the frame to support an iron bikini.

Gaming is in his blood. My husband and his brothers grew up as gamers. While their father encouraged them to go get some fresh air, Malcolm and his brothers remained loyally indoors with their Nintendo. The only video games I ever played as a kid were ones like *King's Quest* and the *Olympics* on my high-tech PC jr. So I'm not so much what one might call a *gamer*—even though I won a whole lot of gold medals for the USA "running" track.

I've tried not to take it personally. I've tried to understand the allure that the gaming world holds, but I'm just not there. Each time he touches the computer keyboard I'm filled with angst. Sneaky plans step out of the shadows of my mind, and I marvel at how cunning I've become. Vacuums have been known to eat computer power strips from time to time, haven't they? Keyboards can survive a thorough cleaning in the dishwasher, can't they? Computer screens are a perfect place to hang sopping wet jeans to air-dry, right?

For everyone's safety, I don't think I should be left alone with the computer anymore, but I don't have a choice. I'm home alone a lot more than my husband, and from virtually every room in our apartment, I can see my husband's mistress staring at me blankly. I'm always an eye roll away from knowing what my future will hold for the upcoming evening—me watching Mal chat up virtual sorcerers.

My husband swears that he wants to spend time with me, and I always fall for it. I'm sure he does want to spend *some* time with me, I just think his time-spending version and mine are different—his version is shorter.

After work, Malcolm listens to me talking about my day and fills my conversational spaces with the appropriate nods and grunts, but thirty-nine minutes after his arrival, I can see him eyeing his computer console. A dismal longing fills Mal's eyes, and I know deep down that he'd rather be vanquishing squatty trolls than be with me. That hurts.

Even if I really did have the wherewithal to sabotage Mal's game playing, the major glitch is that Malcolm would spot my motive straight away. He already knows I feel slighted by his game playing.

"Mal, can we spend some time *together* tonight?"

"Sure."

"Great! I'll start dinner and then maybe we can watch some *Buffy*? Will you help?"

"Sure, I'll be there in a minute . . ."

My husband got lost on his way to the kitchen.

Malcolm took a major detour to the world of Azeroth, stopping in to say hi to pointy-hatted wizards and buxom women. His one minute turned into five, and then into fifteen; before I realized I had basically prepared the whole dinner solo. Once the stove was turned off, I could hear him talking with his virtual online team instead of with his real in-the-kitchen wife.

I wonder if a computer hard drive can survive relaxing in a bubble bath?

I shouldn't have to remind my husband that he does enjoy spending time with his wife, but inevitably that's exactly what ends up happening.

As calmly as I can, I remind him that he said he was going to help me cook, or watch a movie, or just have a chat. That's when I should probably go put on my evildoer bad-girl cape, but I don't feel like a menace. I feel like a parent. I feel like I'm scolding him. I feel like I'm his dad telling him the sun is shining outside and to stop wasting his precious time on mind-numbing games. I want to feel like *his wife*—a wife who he wants to spend time with.

Like a good wife-parent, I try to be consistent in my needs, but some days I'm just too tired to ask him to turn off the computer, and I let his gaming slide. Then there are some days I really do want him to choose what's going to make him happiest. I want to stop the tug-of-war that's happening between us, so I stop tugging. But after a couple hours of him playing, that supportive-wife facade cracks, and an overpowering need to make my husband pay attention to me seeps in.

I know I'm being greedy. Greedy for more time and more attention. I convince myself that thirty minutes is enough, and then it's not. I know that an hour will be plenty, but then it isn't. I'm like an addict—addicted to my husband's attention. But is that bad? I didn't think it was until I started feeling so empty when our time was up.

What makes it worse is that I know he won't choose more time with me. Then I feel that familiar push and pull begin, and I want to pull Malcolm back to me.

Malcolm and I have surely exhausted this topic. How many more ways can I ask Mal to stop yearning for his game console while we are together? He does try to focus on me (sort of), but even upon returning from a thirty-second trip to the bathroom I find him trying to sneak in some gaming time. Maybe I could get one of his online gamer friends to mention it?

I can see him blowing up castles from my vantage in the kitchen, and I miss him. I miss what we could be. I miss what we should be—together. Mal can tell me over and over again that he *loves* me, and he just *likes* playing games, but I don't believe him. When you love someone, you spend time with them. When you love someone, you stop them from being hurt.

I always thought my husband would do anything for me. It's not any guy who will drive an hour and a half at midnight to see his girlfriend only to give her a hug because her day was horrible. The girl in that story is not a made-up fairy princess. The girl in that story was me. The boy in that story was Malcolm. With that kind of track record I just figured Malcolm would fix anything that needed fixing—especially if he was the one causing it.

I need Malcolm to fix this. I need him to be my husband. I need him to stop playing games.

What does his computer have that I don't? And then I remember—iron-bikini-clad women and bearded trolls. I can't compete with that. I shouldn't have to.

If I stay in this apartment any longer only to watch two-dimensional scantily clad vixens pass before my husband's eyes, I might turn to a life of cybersabotage. Nowhere in this tiny apartment is safe from Mal and his gaming obsession.

Stealthy schemes are taking shape, but there's one that keeps coming up. This one I might actually initiate. I wonder if I could make Mal miss me?

I'm tired of staring at my husband's back, and I'm weary of sitting here waiting for him to pay attention to me. I wonder if my husband would notice if I left and went to a movie? Maybe I should. I think it's time to get my bad-girl cape dry-cleaned, because I am going out! But first, I'll IM him to let him know where I'm headed.

I decide to participate in out-of-the-apartment activities, along with taking a university extension course. My focus changes from Mal to me. My down-with-computers plotting ceases, and strange and new ideas begin appearing in my mind.

Once out of the apartment feeling fancy-free, I can see that I have much more alone time than my husband. I'm always able to find ways to be fully charged by the time he comes home from work. I'm excited to have someone to talk to, and better yet, it is my best friend—my husband. Malcolm does not have the same free-time luxury. This is why he continues to seek the solace of his game console over me.

I had wanted my husband—no, I had *needed* my husband—to be my entire social outlet. I'd wanted my Mal's focus away from his computer and on me. This hadn't seemed like such an outrageous wifely request, but it might be too much to ask all night, every night. It took getting out of the apartment to realize that.

"Malcolm, what are you doing up so early? You have almost two hours before work," I said staring at the clock.

"Oh, I thought I'd get my gaming in now so I can see you when I come home."

Whoa.

Malcolm and I have found more of a balance when it comes to his gaming/recharging time. There are still days I stare at the computer and wonder what would happen if I had a tea party atop his hard drive, but those days happen less and less, and I can tolerate them more and more.

What started out as a way to get back at my husband turned out to be a way to get back to myself. Malcolm came up with a compromise all on his own. My husband had chosen me because I had chosen myself.

CHAPTER 14

Tour L'Amour á la Kitchen

How to meet in the middle
(or at least in the kitchen)

Tonilyn and Michael

I'm having issues—food issues to be precise. These food issues are neither the kind where a person secretly stashes candy in a bottom drawer nor the more serious kind discussed on the OWN Network. These are the kind of food issues where my husband refuses to cook.

In his defense, my husband doesn't outwardly refuse to cook, he just makes himself scarce around dinnertime. If asked to help prepare dinner, my husband is suddenly embroiled in a pressing project that *must* be completed immediately or he *must* watch the end of the exciting football game. What's a hungry wife to do?

Dinnertime somehow morphs our otherwise modern marriage into an iconic Norman Rockwell painting. As husband and wife, we become the round-faced Rockwellian couple happily dining together. However, the more scrutinizing of art devotees would certainly note the atypical grimace lurking quietly behind the wife's adoring eyes. As much as this devoted wife loves her husband, she does not always love cooking for him.

There's something about cooking alone in our kitchen that makes my stomach growl, and it's not because I'm hungry. I don't like cooking and I don't like cooking for my husband—and it's not because I'm a bra-burning feminist either. (There are times when I'd like to burn down my kitchen, but that would just make me an arsonist.)

It is true that a large part of me balks at the traditional feminine role, but I am simply of the belief that we are all created equal. We are all created equal in life, in marriage, and most certainly in the kitchen. Left all alone in a kitchen built for at least two, I feel isolated. I am completely on my own in a world of cold black Teflon and hard wooden spoons. Why do I stay? I'm hungry.

The first few months of our marriage, in our new house, in our new kitchen, I was surprised that my husband and I weren't cooking together every night. I was surprised because truly, we do *everything* together.

My husband is the only person I know who I never tire of being around, so I wanted him in the kitchen with me spilling flour and making wisecracks about chicken breasts. But it was a solo show. It was only then that I really began to see the kitchen as the "woman's place," mainly because I was the only one there. It was then that I began to grow quietly resentful. I wanted my seven nights a week, two shows on Sunday solo act to become a duo. I wanted a cooking partner. I wanted *my* partner.

I started trying whatever I could think of to entice my husband into our kitchen. I thought that if we could take on the care and feeding of each other together, it might quell the resentful monster in my belly. I tried asking him to help me prepare his own favorite meals. I tried starting dinner every evening at the same time in order to create a schedule. All these efforts seemed to lure my wily husband into the kitchen for a night or two, but inevitably he would retreat back to his projects or his football.

I tried reasoning with myself. There are some household tasks that I don't do. I never take out the trash. Only when my husband is out of town do I find myself awkwardly wheeling the large plastic garbage cans to the curb. I never do yard work. My allergies and lack of clipping stamina do me in when trimming trees or hedging hedges.

Without complaint, my husband performs these typically male chores. He doesn't ask for my help and isn't put out that I'm not on trash duty with him. So why am I all bent out of shape because he won't cook with me? This rationalization spell only holds its charm for a few shake-and-bake dinners, and then I'm right back where I started—in the kitchen alone and coming to a slow boil.

Now, if this were my best girlfriend's dilemma, I would immediately counsel her to simply talk with her husband. I would tell her to be honest and communicate her feelings of isolation and frustration. Of course, once my girlfriend had communicated all of this misplaced hurt and resentment, her husband would instantly apologize and all would be well. We would undoubtedly find this changed husband in the kitchen rustling up some dinner that very same evening. As Dr. Phil is fond of saying, "You teach people how to treat you."

I must be the worst teacher. Talking to my husband about my kitchen issues has not yet produced any concrete solution. Just as my feeble attempts to coax him into the kitchen bring a possible two days of kitchen-bliss into my lonely Hamburger Helper world, honestly communicating my feelings of isolation and frustration has brought about the same two-day result. The only difference being that a lovely apology precedes the hamburger helping.

"I just don't understand why you don't want to help me cook," I say again to my husband before I start dinner one evening.

"It's not that I don't want to help you cook . . . I just don't think about eating . . .," my husband explains.

My husband's candid admittance suddenly makes my own feelings crystal clear. My frustration and confusion melt away, and I understand. Why have I so desperately wanted a cooking partner in that kitchen? Why have I been so bent out of shape because my husband won't cook with me? I feel forgotten. "I just don't think about eating . . ." translates as, "I just don't think about you. . . ." I have been feeling like an unloved cook. I want to feel like a loved wife. I want to feel like a family.

My entire childhood, I witnessed my mom and dad cooking together in the kitchen. At family holidays, my parents, grandparents, my sister, and I all gathered in the kitchen to help prepare our meals. Even if only one person was cooking, the rest of us would offer to set the table or pour drinks or something to help.

It was never about the actual dish being prepared or the act of cooking. It was always about the teamwork. It was always about being a family. That sense of family baked its way into my heart. As a married adult, I have been looking for that same sense of kitchen-love in my new kitchen with my husband. It isn't just the heat of the stove that gives the kitchen its warmth—it's the love of the family cooking in it.

I now understand that my husband never meant to be hurtful or dismissive in his kitchen avoidance. For my husband, cooking is simply about eating—no more, no less. I get now that for me, cooking is about so much more. In my kitchen, cooking is about teamwork and family love and all things sugary sweet and gooey.

I'm still happiest in our kitchen on the nights my husband wanders in to help me cook. On those nights, the food tastes sweeter and the kitchen feels warmer. On those nights, the angry rumbling in my belly abates and it feels full—of gooey, warm, kitchen-love.

So it would seem that our cheerful Rockwellian couple still makes appearances at our dining room table. However, the ever-observant art lover might now notice something different hidden in the depths of that same wife's eyes. That scowling grimace has finally been replaced with something a little lighter and a whole lot gooier—understanding. That understanding doesn't bring my husband into the kitchen with me, but that understanding does bring me into the kitchen differently.

CHAPTER 15

Will Trade Sex for Clean Floors

How to "encourage" your husband's inner housekeeper out into your house

Sophie and Nick

I'm almost afraid to pick it up. If I buy it, I'll have to devise some plan to distract the buff dude at the checkout from looking at it too closely. The title doesn't give away too much—*The Sweet Potato Queens' Book of Love*—so I'm safe there. It's what the book is suggesting that makes my face turn pink like an embarrassed teenager about to buy tampons. I'm too old to ask my mom to drive the five hours it takes to get here just to buy me this book (and some more tampons). This is silly. I can do this. Really, I don't have much of a choice. I need answers. At this point I'll try anything.

It's getting worse—my husband's Husband Helplessness. It's a strange condition, and I'm not so sure what brings it on. Being married I guess. I might not know the exact cause, but I can list some of the symptoms: Floors half mopped. Tasks done half-assed or not at all. Red socks in the white laundry. And who's left to pick up the slack? Me.

Nick's latest Husband Helplessness fiasco was not his first household offense. It just happened to be his greatest cleaning blunder. The telltale raspberry-pink-stained load was a dead give-away that his condition had worsened.

Not only had my virgin white bras turned a shade of faded floozy pink, but I couldn't believe my capable husband had made such a huge laundering mistake. Nick has been doing laundry since I told Nick he needed to start doing laundry. How many years has my husband been capably washing and folding, and there's never been an incident of this magnitude?

My husband is testing me.

What if contained in these 240 pages is the answer to this unsolvable problem? What if I walk off without buying it because I'm too much of a prude to at least read further? The bright pink heart on the book's cover reminds me of the floozy pink bra I'm now sporting, and I quietly seethe.

What if this book can set me free?

It's just that according to what I've gleaned from a brief book-store scan, the author is suggesting a very unorthodox, and slightly scandalous, method in order to *encourage* a husband. (I reread the back blurb several times just to make sure this wasn't part of the *50 Shades of Grey* series. It's not.) It's just this: For a gal to get her guy to do *anything*, all the gal has to do is promise something. Something specific. Something men really like. Something men *really really* like. This oh-so-specific promise is not something as simple as ordering your husband his favorite pizza in exchange for help. (I tried that. It doesn't work.) This oh-so-specific promise falls more along the lines of *wearing* your husband's favorite pizza—and nothing else.

The fact that I haven't yet put this book back on the shelf says that I'm either at my wits end or more of a sexual deviant than I thought. Boy, Nick's Husband Helplessness is driving me to new and possibly lurid solutions.

Having immediately acquired a pure mind of its own, my right arm quickly places the book back on the shelf. Maybe I should keep using my words at home? It's just that they don't seem to get the job done—no matter how many or what kind I use.

"You know, this used to be white," I said to Nick as I held up the evidence—my once-white bra. "Now it's pink." He looked confused (and a little turned on).

Nick shrugged his shoulders.

"Oh . . .? It was the towels," was his decided response.

Towels?! What towels?

I tried to follow his logic, but I couldn't because there was none.

Honestly, if my husband had countered with any sort of intelligent remark, I might have chalked it up to a onetime mistake and let it go. He could have apologized. He could have acted shocked and surprised. Instead, he acted incompetent—which he is most certainly not. He's trying to sneak out of doing his chores (especially his laundry) by implying he doesn't understand the fundamentals of washing clothes—Husband Helplessness.

My husband is testing me.

My husband is crazy meticulous about his clothes and folds his shirts better than Disney Store employees!

My husband is testing me.

Maybe I should go for a nice romance novel instead of trying to solve this unsolvable marital problem. I'm sure that in the book *A Hunger Like None Other*, the heroine's romantic interest empties the dishwasher while doing all his own laundry. And I can't imagine the buxom woman standing next to Fabio on the cover of *You Sex Devil* having a conversation about red socks, white bras, and floor mopping. (Well, maybe about white bras.)

I could try talking about dry mopping in a sexy way and then maybe Nick would complete his task, but probably not. I have Super Cleaning Vision, because I can see the unevenness of the vacuum trails in the carpet. I can clearly spot the dust huddled in the center of the room. How many times have I mentioned that perimeter sweeping doesn't count? Does my husband think he's that sneaky? Does he really think he's gotten away with doing half the work? He's like a kid trying to weasel his way out of putting away his toys because he suddenly can't find the toy box. Why has marriage made my husband so lazy?

"When you mop the floor, you have to mop the *whole* floor. I know you're smarter than that."

His response is a deeply caring shoulder shrug.

So, I'm thinking that a romance novel is not going to be my best bet right now. Well, this new *system* of encouragement might be good at giving me some ideas. Not that I need any—do I?

It's not like my sex life is lacking in sex. Nick and I are doing fine. I'm sure my husband feels about sex like I feel about gelato—more is always better. If I buy *The Sweet Potato Queens' Book of Love* and try this *method*, he'd probably be getting more, because I'd be getting clean floors and clean laundry. But is trading *favors* worth it?

If one of my best girlfriends told me that she had been exchanging *favors* with her husband for emptying the dishwasher, after the immediate shock wore off, what would I think? Would I judge her? Would I applaud her genius?

I keep thinking of scenarios where it's acceptable marital behavior to barter in this *sexy* way. Then I think of Nick's unacceptable marital behavior, and I'm tempted to strut up to the counter in my floozy-pink bra and buy this book! I might be ready for a cleaning revolution brought on by a sexual one—because that's kind of what the author is suggesting—a wife's own personal sexual uprising.

Nothing is changing at home.

What if this book *is* it?

This floozy-pink bra cutting off my circulation is making me tenser than I already was. I feel like my loving partner is handing me the dust rag, the mop, the vacuum, the laundry basket, the washer, the dryer, the stove, and the refrigerator and saying, "You're the wife. You do it."

The women on the cover of *The Sweet Potato Queens' Book of Love* look so happy and relaxed. If anything, it looks like a fun read. Yes, her viewpoint is *unusual*, and this is of course precisely why I can't stop thinking about it. Kissing my husband and having him magically turn into a handsome prince who vacuums has always been a dream of mine.

I can at least read a little of it.

Maybe the author is really talking about sweet potatoes, and I'm missing the whole point? That's why I should take it home and give it a thorough once-over.

No one will ever have to know but me and the burly dude at the checkout counter. I'll hide it under the bed. Nick will never see it. He never vacuums all the way under there anyway.

Over the years, I've read a lot of self-help books about this very issue. Most of them have provided valuable tools to help me express myself more clearly. I get it. I have to help myself first, and I do that by stating my needs plainly. I've learned to be specific, get to the point, and ask for what I want.

After years of practice, I think I'm pretty good now at the asking. It's just that Nick is not so good at the doing. These books don't seem to cover what to do in case of a stubborn husband. There are two of us living in our house—unless you count our cats as people. Then there are four of us. I know I can't train the cats to dust and mop correctly, so my husband is going to have to pick up their slack.

It's just that Nick's Husband Helplessness feels mean. If this Husband Helplessness happened only every now and then, it would be easier to handle, but my requests feel brushed aside, much like dust on the floor would feel if Nick did his job. Maybe it *would* be easier to teach our cats how to pull their own weight around here. At least someone in our house would be helping.

If this happy book doesn't yield some inspiration, maybe I should just hire a live-in maid. At least that's fair. Then neither of us would be doing anything. Although, the maid might just teach my husband to slack off even more.

"Nick, aren't you going to brush your teeth?"

"Oh, I'm waiting for the maid to help me with that."

Thankfully, though at this point a live-in maid is way out of our budget, this shiny new book is not.

I've tried talking to my husband. I've tried to turn a blind eye to pink bras and rose-colored whites. I've tried not feeling hurt. I need to try something else.

The Sweet Potato Queens' Book of Love is proving *interesting* reading on a vast array of Husband Helplessness subjects. I'm not sure how I feel. I'm not sure it'll work. I wonder if the lovely little old ladies at my church would give me this kind of marital advice. (Then again, they might—their spunk always surprises me.) I wonder—would Nick be mad that I tried to *motivate* him in such a foxy way? And after all is said and done, even though I'd have clean floors, would I feel dirty?

Maybe I could try it just once—more for a social experiment. All in the name if science. What if I can fit the author's *system* into whatever I happen to be in the mood for *giving* that day? Is that wrong? The promise of shiny-clean floors that I don't have to shine is almost too much for me to take. Who'd have to know? I didn't think I'd ever use sex as a weapon per se, but as a cleaning tool—it's worth at least one try.

Following the author's instructions, I walk up to my husband. I state my needs clearly. I promise to be true to my word.

"Sweetheart, I'd really appreciate your help with the house. I promise to **(insert sexual favor here)** if you will clean the floors."

I've never seen a man *run* to get a vacuum.

→HUSBAND RAISING 101←

My husband likes to do things at his own pace. However, when it comes to chores, his own pace is never.

—LILY on her husband's attitude regarding household chores

Living with a roommate can be a challenge—living with your husband can be even more of a challenge. From their husbands' lack of cleaning initiative, to their avoidance of cooking, to figuring out the right amount of influence it takes to "encourage" a husband to pick up a broom, these wives have dealt with their fair share of the classic male stereotypes.

Instead of focusing on their manly annoyances, our heroines chose to look deep within themselves to dust off the truth behind their own frustrations. From this objective standpoint, each wife could then become the catalyst for cleaning up the mess that a lack of mutual respect caused in their otherwise organized marriages.

SKILL BUILDING COVERED IN PART II

- ☐ How to get your husband to organize his toys
- ☐ How to divide household chores and use teamwork to encourage your husband to clean
- ☐ How to understand yourself so that you may better understand your partner
- ☐ How to respect one another's living space
- ☐ How true acceptance itself can solve problems

PART III

FRANKLY MY DEAR, I WANT YOU TO GIVE A DAMN

Bringing Out the Love in Any Situation

CHAPTER 16

Let Them Eat Cake*

How to retain your sense of self while baking

Tonilyn and Michael

My husband loves cake.

Let me clarify—my husband loves *one* kind of cake. The cake he adores isn't just any old run-of-the-mill store-bought cake. Oh no, it's an extremely special cake. This cake has a super-secret recipe that's been handed down from generation to generation.

Like a new medieval wife is handed the kitchen accounts by her mother-in-law, each wife in my husband's family is handed this super-secret vanilla cake recipe. For over sixty years, each wife has happily accepted the passing of the spatula. Each wife but this one.

I've never felt hatred toward any sort of baked good until this cake. Over the years I have grown to loathe this overly sugary vanilla confection so much, I refuse to bake it. My refusal to bake this super-special cake has been a recipe for disaster throughout my entire married life.

*Cake name has been changed to protect the innocent.

"I'm going to teach you how to bake Michael's favorite cake," my mother-in-law, Sue, animatedly informs me one afternoon.

Not wanting to make waves, I agree to an afternoon of baking. I don't mention that I'd never baked a cake in my life. I also neglect to disclose another key fact—I don't enjoy cooking.

I've never experienced the joy of cooking. I cook because I must eat, and my creative process in the kitchen pretty much ends there. There were times in college when I tried to find the joy in stirring and whisking. I wanted to prepare fancy meals for my beaux and impress them with my dessert-making prowess. I wanted to experience that surge of Betty Crocker–like pride, but the feeling never came. I willingly hung up my apron, ordered takeout, and never looked back.

As promised, Sue took me into her kitchen and walked me through the family's super-secret vanilla cake baking process. Sue watched me clumsily breaking eggs and spilling flour all over her kitchen counter.

My hands started trembling as I took hold of the electric mixer for the first time. Batter was flying, butter was melting, and I envisioned myself as June Cleaver in an episode of *Leave it to Beaver.* I was the quintessential mom with perfectly coiffed hair, tiny pearl necklace, and dainty high heels baking in the kitchen. I was the devoted wife and mother, filmed in soft, flawless black and white, doing what was expected of me—creating delicious dinners and grand desserts.

My hands became sweaty, and the plastic handle of the electric mixer grew slippery. The smell of the cake batter fed the butterflies in my stomach and gave them a sugar high. This was not my world. I had always seen myself in flawed living color. I was more comfortable in a *Family Ties* kind of world where there were acid-wash jeans, thick ugly sweaters, and microwaveable dinners. I was more comfortable in a world where roles were not automatically assigned, but discovered. That was where I wanted to live.

Applying icing until my arm might fall off, I began to understand that this cake is filled with more than just eggs and sugar. It's filled with expectation.

"If you loved me, you would bake it," my husband declared one day.

"If you loved me, *you* would bake it," I suggested.

I had to come up with a solution—a recipe Michael and I both could swallow.

"I've been thinking," I began after takeout one evening, "I know how much you love your vanilla cake, and you know how much I hate cooking . . . so maybe it would be fun if we tried baking it together?"

Michael thought.

Michael sighed.

Michael agreed.

It's been nine years, and so far no vanilla cake has graced our oven. However, if it ever does, it won't be because I'm expected to fill a role predetermined for me.

In our relationship, Michael and I each bring our own dishes to the table. That's how I see it. That's my key ingredient for a working and happy marriage. We understand each other enough to know that a balanced mix is required for our relationship to continue to rise—even if the cake never does.

CHAPTER 17

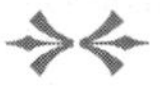

Kid Stuff

How to get your husband to share parental responsibilities

Ellen and Frank

"Frank, I'm so tired. Will you go check on her?"

"What are you, crazy?"

I wait for Frank to finish that sentence with something like, "What are you, crazy? You've been up for forty-eight hours, of course I will," but instead what finishes it is his snoring.

What are you, crazy?

What is *he*, crazy? He must be nuts, because no sane husband would ask a sleep-deprived mother of two that question at 4:44 a.m.

Briefly, I think about jumping up and down on the bed to wake up my snoring husband, but my legs would give out way before Frank would actually wake up. He's a deep sleeper, and I can barely summon enough energy to blink, let alone jump.

Tomorrow morning all three of us would have a little talk, though—me, Frank, and his psyche. I'd go crazy on Frank tomorrow. Amy needed me now.

With every ounce of motherly strength I can summon, I start the long trek into the room next door. I feel like I'm swimming through thick air—I need some sleep. I need some help. A night off would be nice.

What are you, crazy?

Like a flash of lightning followed by Frank's thunderous snores comes The Thought. The Thought that keeps popping into my head: I am crazy. I'm crazy to ask my husband for help.

I'm the parent on call. Daytimes and evenings I'm right there—especially evenings. Nighttime parenting always falls to me, because my husband is dead to the world once he falls asleep. Poking him, saying his name, one of our girls crying, or my shouting "Frank, there's a fire!" are all ways *not* to wake up my husband.

A sniffle, a whimper, or a small cry from the kids' room immediately jolts me awake while Frank happily finishes dreaming of gorging himself at an all-you-can-eat french bread bar. (The Mom Club forgot to warn me that super hearing also comes along with super stretch marks.)

I don't think I've had a full night's sleep or an uninterrupted shower in over five years. Now that we have a second little girl, do I have to wait five more years to be clean?

This week I've already missed four full showers and four full evenings of David Letterman because my girls have been sick. Amy's been sick the past two days, which in and of itself wouldn't be that bad except that her older sister Jenny was sick the two days before that.

Between work and being up at all hours over the last four days I've averaged two hours of sleep a night—if that. Seems like tonight's going to be no exception. I hope sleep deprivation doesn't lead me to do something truly crazy, like grill the puppy and walk the hamburgers, because at the moment I'm so tired I want to curl up into a ball and bawl.

I knew that having two kids was going to be tough. There would be sleepless nights, and I might get lost in a sea of wet wipes and poopy diapers. However, I assumed that my husband would dive into the deep end with me. There has been no diving. I'm a single mom—with a husband. I had no idea I'd be doing this all alone, but what's worse is that I've only myself (and my husband's sleepy subconscious) to blame.

The day we brought Jenny home from the hospital is the day I scooted Frank over to the side. From day one, I took over. I took over because I knew what to do, and Frank was too slow to come to our rescue.

"Why is she crying? Should I feed her? Should I change her diaper? Should I hold her?"

His questions never inspired a lot of confidence in his parenting ability. I thought I'd just let him stick to the occasional diaper change and tea party invite. That seemed safer.

I must have been crazy.

All those years I stepped up while Frank sat down. I never insisted that Frank help. And he never insisted on helping. It's not like he pushes me out of the way when I change Jenny's vomit-soaked shirt or becomes irate if I decide to take over his evening feeding duties. I never felt completely comfortable giving him his Baby Operator's License. It's like I'd be giving him a license to operate heavy machinery when he's never even sat in a tractor. So, if I do ask Frank to help, I try to keep it simple with favors like putting away the clean dishes or picking the Play-Doh out of the carpet. Each time I ask him, he asks me, "Can you wait a second?" No. I can't. I just end up doing it myself because it has to be done—because it's easier.

I must have been crazy.

I should have let him try a little harder. I should have taken the time to show him how to properly change a diaper, warm the bottle, or given him a carefully detailed list explaining all of Jenny's twenty-six different cries. Had I done that, when Amy came along her father would have been ready to share the load. What will Frank do when I ask for his help now? His "can you wait a second?" has lasted over five years.

I was crazy. I was crazy not letting my girls' father be their father.

I can barely make out the alarm beeping over my husband's snores. Thank goodness the girls are finally sleeping, because Frank and I need to have a little chat—pronto. I can't wait all day. That *would* make me go crazy.

Frank is going to have to give up some quality Frank time for some Dad time. Frank might even have to sacrifice some quality evening programming to help get the girls ready for bed. Frank is definitely going to have to take one night a week and spend the entire evening alone with his kids, so I can spend an entire evening with myself. Will Frank survive?

"You're up?" Frank asks as I drag myself into our bedroom. It would seem he has no memory of last night.

"I am. So, last night when I asked you to check on Amy because she was crying, you said 'Are you crazy?'"

Frank laughed.

"No, I didn't. There's no way I would have said that."

"You did."

Too tired to get mad and too raw to give him a long list of how much I do compared with how much he does not do, I simply said, "This has to change."

I could feel the energy of the room shift. Maybe it was my fatigue adding such a weight to my words, but mostly I think it was the seriousness of my tone that added the heaviness. If Frank didn't hear me in this moment, he might very well come home to a crazy hamburger-walking wife.

Frank didn't move.

"I need for you to give me a night off. I need for you to help with the girls more. I need you to help me—you're their father." With that last statement, I felt like crying. But my tears must have been off sleeping, because none came.

Frank must have heard my "I am done" tone and known that to argue at this juncture would have been a poor move on his part. He couldn't have been more right. Had he said anything to the contrary, I would have found the energy somewhere deep inside and gone crazy on him.

"All right," was all Frank said.

That seemed easy enough, but I knew this wasn't the only conversation we'd have. It was a first step—if a good one.

I threw the comforter over my head and listened to my husband's shower. I wondered if Frank was nervous about what this all meant. What if he was resistant? What if he came up with excuses or felt his tennis match was more important than giving his wife some quality time?

If that happened, I'd just have to insist. I'd insist on his help from now on.

This meant that I'd have to let Frank make some mistakes. Hopefully his mistakes would be minor, and I wouldn't come home to Jenny finger painting her baby sister or a Slip 'N Slide in the living room. I'd have to let Frank learn to be a dad. That was not going to be so easy, but right now I'd let Frank take the kids to work if that would get me three more minutes of sleep.

I must have dozed off, because when I opened my eyes Frank was dressed in his suit and ready to leave.

He kissed my forehead goodbye, but before I heard the front door close, I heard him quietly walk into the girls room to check on them.

This will work.

Now maybe I can sleep.

For five years.

CHAPTER 18

The Husbandry of Mind Reading

How to read your husband's mind. (I knew you were going to say that.)

Lily and Gus

My husband thinks I'm psychic. I, for one, was shocked to discover this—both that I'm psychic, and that my husband believes me to be thus. True, I am able to predict with astounding accuracy my morning doughnut craving. However, I still don't think it prudent to hang out a Psychic Reader sign just yet. I need more proof. Luckily, my husband is providing that for me.

Gus has so much faith in my soothsaying talents that he is aiding me in my psychic education. My husband is helping me by *not* telling me how he feels. Like a sage mind reader, I'm just supposed to know. I'm thinking of investing in a crystal ball, because so far I'm terrible at reading my husband's mind.

Somewhere along the line, I had hurt him. I had hurt him badly. His statement made that abundantly clear. I could feel my husband's resentment explode with the pent-up rage of a deranged stage mom from *Toddlers & Tiaras*. How was I to know he was mad?! I'm not a mind reader! Oh right—forgot. I'm supposed to be.

The last time I had a deep conversation in a movie theater parking lot I was a teenager. Sadly, the adult conversation that Gus was starting now did not involve giggly hair-flipping or an intense exposition regarding the character assassination of Marcus Brody in *Indiana Jones and the Last Crusade*.

"You don't support me!" Gus angrily accused. What had started out as lovely movie date night had devolved into this scene.

I was blindsided.

This was all going too fast. I needed time to focus. How could my husband expect me to harness my great mind-reading capabilities in a noisy AMC parking lot? I needed quiet. I needed tea leaves. I needed a *real* psychic.

Wait! Hold everything! I can feel a prediction coming on! Yes, yes, with great confidence I can predict that this dramatic husband and wife scene is going to get good. Too bad I've eaten all my Twizzlers.

I stared at my husband. My husband's usual sensitive calmness had turned bristly and rough like a kitchen scouring pad. Even with the help of an XXXL super-sized crystal ball, a creepy magic mirror on the wall, the ghost of Nostradamus, and a translator to understand the French-speaking ghost of Nostradamus, I am confident I could not have predicted this latest blowout.

Instead of using my mighty powers of mind reading, I opted for my stronger powers of wifely deduction. Thinking back, I struggled to find a hint of what could have changed so dramatically.

Like a misty vision, the last several weeks slowly came into focus. I recognized the weeks of stiffness. I saw the days of quiet, frustrated looks in my direction. (Ooh, I remembered where I hid my last doughnut!) It was clear that Gus' resentment had been simmering for a while. Had my husband been silently stewing?

All signs point to yes.

The clues had been subtle. Even the most expert of wives might have missed the signs. An abrupt hang-up. A curt exchange.

A series of one-word answers. Gus had been closed off. He'd been an impenetrable fortress. I'd missed the clues.

It doesn't take a great psychic to read my husband's mind. It just takes an observant wife. If I hear my husband yelling from the dining room, in my mind's eye I can "see" that the computer has crashed. If I don't receive a casual "Good morning" greeting, I can "predict" he has not had his morning coffee. If my husband has holed up in the basement all evening, I "know" his golf score was 130+ that day. I think these "predictions" may have more to do with knowing my husband than my actual soothsaying prowess.

How had I missed the simmering and the smoldering and the seething? Well, I left my magic wand at the movie theater when we went to see the last *Harry Potter* movie, so I was unable to *accio* my mind-reading bonnet—obviously. Or I hadn't been paying attention.

In my mind, there were many reasonable reasons for Gus' strange strangeness. He was busy. He was tired. He was focused. All of these explanations seemed plausible.

Gus had been under a lot of stress, and stress can render even the most delightful of people somber and aloof. My actor husband had been in all-day rehearsals for weeks, opening two shows in three months. I understood it. I supported it. I thought I was being a good wife by giving him space to focus and work.

Be it due to my innate stinginess when it comes to investing in a real crystal ball instead of a spongy Nerf one or my inherent inability to read minds, this time around my spidey-sense was not attuned to Gus' subtle shifts—not even close. My wife radar had failed, and I need to return my soothsaying cards back to the cereal box from whence they came.

I had missed the signs. Why? Because my husband never held up one. My husband may think I'm psychic, but I am not a mind reader.

I trust my husband to talk to me. Not just about his love for *Downton Abbey* or his crappy day at the driving range—I trust him to tell me the colossal stuff as well. I want my husband to tell me if he's mad or angry or just won the lottery. This way we can work through life together. We can decide as a couple to handle whatever life throws our way. If we aren't talking about life and our relationship, we aren't giving each other the opportunity to grow and change. We can't decide how to spend the $1.4 million Powerball! These are important things!

I had hoped Gus would choose to share instead of stew. But Gus chose to stew.

"You don't support me," he went on, "I opened two shows, and you did nothing."

Nope. Couldn't have predicted that.

Gus' last show had closed weeks earlier—his first one opened over two months ago. Had he been mad for that long? My paranormal powers are on the fritz. Is there a way to get a tune-up for that? (Is that something the Geek Squad can fix? Seriously, I think those guys can fix anything.)

I stood there quietly while Gus vented. I wanted to cut him off and tell him that he was being ridiculous—of course, I support him. I'm his wife and that's what wives do! I wanted to come to my rescue. I wanted to stop feeling like this was all my fault.

I didn't say a word. I learned early on that letting Gus talk until his heart was empty was the best hope we had of a quick reconciliation—and that's ultimately what I wanted. I'd get my chance to talk, so right now I'd give him his.

Standing in the brightly lit parking lot, I felt like the street lamp was purposely shining a spotlight on my inadequacies. Still, I listened.

Gus softened, "You didn't even come see me in either of my shows . . ."

That was it. That was where the resentment had been born. That was how I had hurt him. Of course, I hadn't intended to hurt my husband. I hadn't purposely withheld my opening night presence like he had purposely withheld his opening night angst.

Gus had opened and closed two shows. I hadn't gone to see them. I hadn't gone to see them because I was in a show. I hadn't gone to see them because Gus was working out of town—seven hours out of town. It seemed impractical for me to go. I'd have to put in for time away from my show, and then drive my tired self seven hours there and seven hours back all within a mere three days of vacation time.

I thought he'd understood. I thought that he had known I would have come if I could have. Gus' silence in the matter had just served to affirm the fact that he supported my decision to stay. I figured he knew the score and this is why he never said anything to the contrary. I figured wrong.

My outlook was not good.

Gus finished his soliloquy. His shoulders relaxed, and I could see him breathing easier.

It was my turn.

"I had no idea you were upset because I didn't come. To me all of this is just work . . ."

Theater is our job. This is what we do for our living. It's just work. It wasn't a big deal. Gus had two opening nights come and go, and it's true—I'd done nothing. I'd not upheld the ancient opening night rites by sending flowers or a card because it wasn't something I thought of as important. I think I probably called and told him to break a leg, but I couldn't be sure. I'd have to check my crystal ball or my cell phone records.

"I'm sorry. Opening nights just aren't important to me," I clarified.

My explanation did not seem to placate him in the least. I could see his body tense.

"But to me . . ." Gus pointedly continued, "they are important. It's important to me."

Now I knew what my husband had been thinking all along. I knew because he had used his out-loud voice. For me, the opening night of a show wasn't that big of a deal. For my husband, opening nights were special, and he wanted to share the magic with his wife. I got it. I understood. I could make an effort to be there. I could make an effort to send flowers. It was important to him, and that trumped my "I don't care" attitude.

"I'm sorry I missed your shows." I saw that he was listening. "I understand it's important to you. Next time, I'll be there."

I could feel the frustration ebb away. My calm, sensitive man was making his way back to center stage.

I'll completely concede that I missed the weeks of silent signs. I'll even go so far as to say I had been slightly callous in my dismissal of his mood as of late. If I can admit to my mistakes, I hope that my husband will finally, once and for all, admit that I am not psychic. I am not a mind reader!

"Gus, please," I asked, ". . . next time—talk to me. I can't read your mind."

Gus nodded.

And in that moment I *could* read his mind—he understood.

CHAPTER 19

The Marriage Sommelier

How to reignite a loving connection in your marriage

Sophie and Nick

I remember when my husband laughed at my jokes. Once my punch line was successfully delivered, Nick would sigh with an amused grin. His quiet chuckle never filled the room, but I wasn't going for the big laugh. I was going for his goofy response. I adored the way he smiled at me. I loved the way his eyes sparkled—delighting in my silliness. I felt special. I felt loved. I felt like my husband and I were truly connected. My husband doesn't laugh at my jokes anymore. And they're *funny*. This is not good.

"How do you get a talkative shirt to be quiet?"

Wait for it.

"Button it up."

Nick is too tired to laugh. Nick is too tired to listen. Nick is too tired to have a wife.

My husband is exhausted when he's home. He spends extra-long days at work, and in the evenings when he's all mine, I'm met with an empty shell. I get it. Nick wants to impress his work colleagues on this new project. I totally get it. What I don't get are loving words, little kisses, or even a tiny smile.

I don't remember the last time I saw Nick truly smile. (Maybe one day, while Nick was in mid-grimace, a coworker hit him on the back and his face stuck that way.) Nick comes home, slumps into his chair, and never raises his head. This is how my husband spends his nights with me.

I spend my evenings rather differently. I put on a show. This show is for one person and one person only—my husband. I try anything and everything to draw his attention out of that chair—good food, good company, good conversation. All good things a good wife can provide. This nightly performance comes complete with wardrobe changes and subtle phrases like, "Do you mind if I slip into something more comfortable?" Nick never minds. Nick never looks up from his man-chair.

Once he's in the arms of that chair, I've lost Nick to an inner world of staring blankly and TV channel changing. Nothing takes his attention away from those engrossing mind-bending activities. Once I even replaced the remote with my hand, trying to encourage a little hand-holding affection. Nick was onto me. My hand doesn't change the TV channels as effectively. We aren't connecting. The only thing Nick is connecting with is that chair—through his butt. I don't hear the chair trying to spark a nice conversation. I don't hear the chair desperately asking him questions about his day, about my day, about the mailman's day.

Nick used to know how to conjugate verbs and create full sentences, like "How are you?" or "You are looking great!" or "Would you like to see a movie?" Complex sentences have become a thing of the past, only to be replaced by a series of dulcet grunts.

"Sweetheart, what fish are the most valuable?"

"Hmm?"

"Goldfish!"

"Hmm."

At least my husband is alive in there somewhere. But other than the odd mumbled grunt, Nick doesn't speak.

Sitting with Nick in the evenings makes me feel like an intruder in my own marriage. I don't feel close to my husband while sitting in stone-cold silence from dinner to bedtime. I look at him, lifeless in that big chair, and I yearn for the man I married. I want to feel his eyes on me. I want to see him looking at me like I'm everything he ever needed. I want the guy back who laughed at my dumb jokes. I want to hear him say something—anything. I'd settle for, "Could you pass the remote?" I miss my husband.

I almost wish we were fighting. If we were arguing, maybe I'd feel like I existed. If we were fighting, something I said would have been regarded as important enough for my husband to talk back to me. But Nick and I aren't fighting. Nick and I aren't doing anything—that's the problem.

What happens if I stop trying to keep us together? I'm scared that if I totally give up, Nick and I will grow so far apart that we won't be able to find our way back, because usually, at some point during the evening, I stop trying to coax my husband out of his shell. I surrender the desperate want to connect with him. Instead, I try connecting with myself. That's when I can feel the sadness wash over me. I feel alone in my marriage. I feel empty. This is how the descent starts. I know it in my bones.

My husband and I are quietly drowning—drifting apart—and I am the only one who notices. We're growing apart because I'm growing apart from my husband. My marriage is not working.

I truly believed that after a couple of months all this would stop. Once Nick understood how to manage his energy at his new job, he would save some for his wife. I was wrong. I'm not sure how we can go on as a couple when we aren't acting like one.

"I feel like we aren't connecting," I confided one night at dinner.

Nick's face went from red to ash in a second. I thought it was the wine turning his cheeks that rosy color, but the look in his eyes betrayed him. I knew it had been my truth. I had terrified him.

It's said that when faced with a scary danger, animals have two instinctual choices—fight or flight. My husband wanted to accrue some frequent flyer miles, because he opted for the flight alternative. He didn't go anywhere—physically. Night after night he was still in that chair. Emotionally, he was more distant than ever. I felt insignificant in a place where I wanted to feel like I mattered. How could Nick ignore the love of his life? How could he sit there and not see me trying so hard to save us? The waves were rising, and we would surely drown.

I had hoped that telling the truth would unlock some hidden magic in our relationship. I had hoped that Nick would summon some inner romance that he had saved away for a rainy day, but shockingly, nothing changed. Dog tired, my husband would arrive home, force a smile, and collapse into his chair.

Weeks went by and I waited. I tried to understand why our life hadn't changed for the better. It seemed like my plea for help had come across as something negative—like a criticism. Because now along with tired, Nick was hopeless. It was like I looked at him and said, "Nick, you are a failure as a husband." I'm not sure how "I feel like we aren't connecting" translates as "You're a failure," but my husband's whole demeanor shouted defeat. I was completely alone in my crusade to save us from The Nothing that was sure to swallow us whole.

I'm not sure I could work on my marriage by myself. There are two of us, and if only one of us was trying, would that work? I wanted my husband to *want* to work with me on us! That's why I spent all those months trying to sweet-talk Nick out of that chair, because we were well on our way to becoming that couple who never speak, that couple who are not a couple, that couple who start out in a fixable rut, but then wake up twenty years later to a mountain of resentment and anger. We would slowly begin to hate each other. I could already feel my anger rising. I could feel it sitting there just waiting for a release. I couldn't let that happen. If I was the only one who recognized the early warning signs, so be it.

It was up to me to work on my marriage—alone. I wasn't sure how that would go, but someone had to step up. Apparently, that someone was me. I felt my resentment building, but that wasn't going to help me save my marriage. I knew if I let my anger eat me up, our marriage would end in disaster. I was desperate enough to try anything to reignite the fires of connection between us.

I began coming up with ideas to foster our connection. First, I went the road most traveled: I begged my husband to take a dance class. That was a no—even after I explained I would be going *with* him. I got creative: I asked him to read to me. At least I could hear his voice. That lasted a couple weeks. (Did Harry ever kill Voldemort?) I became practical: I went to counseling. Alone. That helped me, but I still came home to a zombie. I started praying for a miracle.

Nick was on board with none of my connection-inducing schemes. Maybe my thinking was off. So I tried to come up with things he liked that we could do together instead of something I liked that we could do together. If Nick wasn't going to take my path with me, then perhaps I could walk his road with him. There had to be *something* he liked that would cultivate a connection. Staring blankly at the TV did nothing to help with our closeness, so I had to come up with a better idea.

Something balanced.

Something brilliant.

Something robust.

Nick sat down to dinner. I handed him a book—*Wine for Dummies*.

"Sweetheart, would you mind reading about our wine while I pour it?" I asked innocently.

I saw it. Nick's eyes lit up as he flipped from page to page. I had actually gotten his attention.

Nick had shown a remote interest in wine when we went out to dinner. I thought that maybe his interest just needed to be sparked a little. He had also shown a remote interest in my knitting, but I didn't think having him read from *Knitting for Dummies* would spark anything but eye rolling. If this *Wine for Dummies* ploy didn't work, then knitting might be next. I hoped my umpteenth stab in the dark would take.

As Nick began reading about our wine, his voice had a quality I hadn't heard in quite some time—life. Now and again, he looked up from the page to make sure I was listening. My dispassionate husband was finding his excited voice. Could this be it? Had I finally hit on something we could share?

Alcohol saved my marriage—a bold but true statement. It's also true that after a few glasses of wine my husband suddenly looked like George Clooney, but that's not what saved us. Not even close. I had no idea that night would change our marriage so drastically. I knew my husband enjoyed a glass of wine now and again, but I never would have guessed I had ignited such a passion.

Nick began to read about our wine at dinner. For him it was a great way to shake off the stress of work. Learning something new gave him a little extra energy, and each night Nick could escape into the interesting and unknown. For me, it was a great escape into us. We had finally found something that we both liked and could share together. My miracle had occurred. My prayers had been answered.

Since that night, wine has become a big part of our lives. As a couple, we go to wine tastings. We've traveled far and wide to wineries. Not only are we sharing bottles of wine together, but we are sharing our lives. Nick has finally come out of his shell, and it's not because he's intoxicated. (Well, intoxicated with love for me perhaps.) It's amazing how a pint-sized idea and one tiny glass of vino saved us. And the best part? He's laughing at my jokes again . . .

"Nick, what did the grape say when it got stepped on?"

"Hmmm. What did the grape say when it got stepped on?"

"Nothing—but it let out a little whine."

Nick shook his head and flashed his gorgeous smile in my direction.

I had my husband back.

CHAPTER 20

The Football Widow

How to feel important in your partnership

Tonilyn and Michael

The autumn wind is a cow that wanders the barren plain,
Seeking a helmeted Cowboy over whom to reign.
He dominates the Sundays making man aloof,
No more the doting husbands, off they saunter, hand in hoof.

Professional football in America is a remarkable game. It is an extraordinary game. The men who play it make it so. The men who watch it make it so. The women who lose their men lament it so.

Hello, my name is Tonilyn, and I am a football widow.

In my youth, I'd heard tales of this bedeviled race of menfolk who loved sports above all other things, but I was a naysayer. I was not a true believer. I was not a true believer because I had never witnessed the power that eleven padded men and a ball fashioned of pigskin could wield. I had not yet witnessed this power because I had not yet met my husband.

My husband Michael is a Dallas Cowboys fan. When I mention this in casual conversation, those enlightened few smile knowingly and nod their heads in a reverent bow—I need not say another word. To the those who don't have the slightest idea what a statement like "My husband loves the Dallas Cowboys" means, let me share my knowledge: I have learned that a relationship with one's football team is an intensely sacred pact not easily broken. At the core of this man-plus-team relationship is an unwavering love and devotion that would put some man-plus-woman relationships to shame.

Michael would never dream of courting another team more fair or winning. My husband's heart remains ever steadfast and true. For my part, however, there have been occasions when Michael's staunch love for his "Boys" has led me to wonder if there's enough room in his heart for his "girl."

It's not like I was immediately put out by Michael's fandom. Michael and I met in the fall and began dating in the winter. I quickly came to understand that being in love with Michael also meant being in love with the Dallas Cowboys. So, I decided I was going to be that one-in-a-million supportive girlfriend who loved her boyfriend's sports team as much as she loved her boyfriend. I figured that decision would score me some *major* girlfriend points.

At 8 a.m. every Sunday morning I sleepily donned my required star-studded regalia and went over to Michael's to watch the FOX pregame show. I laughed when Michael laughed, groaned when Michael groaned, and pretended to understand what these jokesters were actually talking about. During the game I was just as lost, so again I followed Michael's lead and cheered when he cheered, cursed when he cursed, and did my girlie best to keep up.

I really tried to catch Michael's football fever. I was immune. Still, each and every Sunday evening, I waited patiently for all my girlfriend points to be tallied up—but they never were. My plan was not working.

I never scored major girlfriend points. I never scored any points. The only thing I did score was an unwanted superpower. For the two hours of pregame chatter, the three to four hours of the game, and the two hours of postgame highlights, I was invisible. I did not exist. My overzealous laughing, cheering, and halfhearted cursing did nothing to prove my existence. Michael never heard me. I could have ridden a unicycle through the house in hot pink pasties and a thong and Michael's head would not have turned. (Okay . . . he *might* have noticed the unicycle.) Being invisible might be a cool superpower to have, but being invisible in a relationship, even for a day, doesn't feel so cool—I felt ignored. I felt unimportant.

I reasoned that I was being totally overdramatic. Because seriously, why couldn't I survive one or two days a week without my boyfriend's undivided attention? Still, on any given Sunday, I felt benched. It left me wondering if Michael was that passionately invested in me.

I was determined to prove that I was important every day of the week. I struggled with how to mention all these feelings in a way that wouldn't seem like I was being an unsportsmanlike girlfriend. I was afraid that Michael would think I was trying to lure him away from his first love, so instead of having an open heart-to-heart talk, I decided to take a different route—a slightly more sneaky route. I hinted.

"Honey, how would you like me to take you out for a romantic dinner? You pick."

"Oh, we can do that later. Football's on."

"Oh HONEY!!! There's a special showing of *Pearl Harbor* at the IMAX today! Want me to take you?"

"Oh, we can do that later. Football's on."

"Honey, there's a new strip club that opened up down the street . . ."

"Oh, *can* we do that later? Football's on."

Hinting never played out—ever. Dinner dates, Michael Bay movies, and even strip clubs weren't enough to lure him away from the TV on game day. (Seriously, though, I never actually offered to take him to a strip club. There would've been no point. He would've chosen football.) Presenting Michael with the opportunity to choose me over his Cowboys never quite played out the way I hoped. I was always getting sacked—and not the way I wanted.

Almost more depressing than coming in second place to a bunch of grisly guys was that I began to feel like I was morphing into something different—something ugly. I feared I was changing into *that* woman. You know *that* woman. *That* woman who totally loathes her man's obsessive sports-loving tendencies. *That* woman who feels her man loves his sports team more than he loves her. *That* woman who stands in the kitchen at a party, complete with cosmo in hand, yammering to anyone within earshot, about how hateful her man is because he vanishes every Sunday. I never wanted to become *that* woman. I never wanted to be that kind of petulant partner. I never wanted to be that cliché.

"My husband loves football more than he loves me! That's wrong! DON'T YOU THINK?!" I shrieked at the checkout guy in Whole Foods.

So now I was a stereotype who was also well on her way to becoming a woman who "hinted" instead of powerfully giving voice to her feelings. This was not who I wanted to be. It was obvious that Michael wasn't going to tire of his beloved Cowboys anytime soon. Clearly this team was very important to him, and clearly I didn't get it. It just didn't make sense to me that a sports game projected on a hard unfeeling television set could take precedence over a warm, loving blonde with a totally killer body. (Okay, I exaggerate . . . I'm not blonde.) I was now as obsessed with Michael's Cowboys as he was, and it certainly wasn't to root for them. So, I decided to take on the entire city of Dallas and her sacred Cowboys for my love's affection. I so wanted to beat those damn Cowboys. I wanted to win. I needed to win.

Sitting on Michael's couch watching him watch the game Sunday after Sunday just served to make me feel less and less important. It felt like all week long the two of us were in an awesome loving relationship, but then magically every Sunday, Michael became a freewheelin' bachelor. Every Sunday when Michael stepped into Bachelorville, I wanted to drag him back into Relationshipland with me. That never worked. Michael's continued Cowboys choice fed that tiny unsure part of me that whispered, "You aren't important. See, he won't even turn off the television set for you." I desperately wanted Michael to prove that tiny voice wrong.

But over the game day TV announcers and Michael's excited screams, I didn't recognize that tiny insecure voice as my own. Was it Michael's job to silence that tiny insecure voice? Or was it mine? Or really, was it Terry Bradshaw's?

I came up with another plan. I decided to take Sundays off. I wanted me back. The me that existed before the Dallas Cowboys and Football Sundays.

Initially, this was not the easiest plan, as it seemed to go against everything I really wanted. I really wanted to spend Sundays with my boyfriend. I had thought that if I stuck by him all day every Sunday eventually he would have to notice me, but that certainly hadn't happened.

It was hard not seeing Michael on one of my only days off, but I stuck to my plan. I began to have fun on my own again. I began to forget about Emmitt Smith and Jerry Jones and T.O. dancing on the center star at Cowboys Stadium. (Okay, no one can ever really forget that.) I had lunch with friends, went shopping, and watched girly programs on TV. I did those things that I liked doing and I did them for me—not for the Cowboys and not for the attention of my boyfriend.

With every passing Sunday I began to feel more like myself again. Ejecting myself from the field of play had worked. I had won. Michael could keep his beloved team. I would keep myself.

Almost more amazing than my own personal epiphany is that once I found my independent important self again, Michael actually began to emerge here and there from Bachelorville and wonder where I was. I couldn't believe it. He started remembering that I existed on Sundays.

"Hey, where are you? Aren't you coming over to watch the game?" Michael would asked enthusiastically.

"I hadn't planned on it," I would reply a little stunned.

"Oh . . . it's just . . . I like watching the game with you. I miss you when you're not here," he would add quietly.

I still don't completely understand why this game wields such power over my husband, but I've stopped trying to figure it out. It's just one of those things.

It's like when I try to explain to Michael why Steve Madden wields such power over my feet. No matter how much I try to explain that these shoes are very different (and more beautiful) than any other pair I own, Michael always responds with a confused, "But don't you already have a pair?" And while I don't totally understand why Michael likes me to wear the same Halloween costume every year, I accept that my wearing it means a lot to him. Besides, my new Steve Madden shoes always look so great with the Dallas Cowboys cheerleader uniform.

CHAPTER 21

Not Waiting for Waits

How to stay true to yourself when your husband wants you to stay true to him

Christine and Danny

"Do you like it?"

Ha! I was so on to him.

"No, it's not really my favorite . . ." my voice trailed off as I watched Danny gently remove the unlabeled CD from the player. I knew what he was doing.

"So, you liked it a *little*?" he prompted.

I marveled at my husband's tenacity. His determination after all these years was pretty incredible. His was a calculated attempt to make me blunder. One misstep and I'd never live it down, but I knew this soon-to-fail-scheme was just another sneaky step in his "clever" plan.

"You like it?"

I recognized the singer's "unique" vocal quality immediately. I have ears that can hear.

"Nope." I was direct. "I didn't like it. Sorry."

Danny put the CD back in the stack with a tiny glare—foiled again.

I was being honest: I didn't like it. Still, I felt compelled to add that patronizing "Sorry" at the end of my sentence. The problem is I wasn't sorry. Not in the least. The bigger problem is we both knew it.

My husband has taken great pains to educate me in the classics—Pac-Man, Galaga, and Space Invaders. Video games are one of his many passions. My husband is passionate about sharing his passions, and he wants to be able to share all he loves with me. Not the least of which is his passion for Tom Waits' music. The problem is that I don't love it. I never have, and I'm not Wait-ing around to love it either.

Usually, I'm more than happy to share in what my husband loves because I can appreciate what he loves. There have even been some cases where I've taken a second look at things simply due to Danny's exuberance. Miraculously, my apathetic view toward baseball changed when I started seeing the games through Danny's eyes. Now we enjoy watching together—something I never in a million years thought would happen.

Seeing life through my husband's eyes can be fun and different, but hearing life through my husband's ears can be painful and annoying. We love a lot of the same singer/songwriters, but Tom Waits has never topped my charts. Our vastly differing opinions on this matter are a musical chasm that none can cross.

I'd been introduced to Mr. Waits years before Danny first confessed his love for me by a campfire, and I didn't love him (Mr. Waits. Not Danny). So, on one of our very first official dates (with Danny not Mr. Waits), when he popped in a CD and told me this was his favorite singer, I recognized the affected tone straight away.

"He's great isn't he? So, you love him?!"

"No. Not really," I confessed. "I've never really liked Tom Waits. Is that a problem?"

It was a problem. It was a problem because I didn't love Tom, and it was a problem because we missed our movie. Danny was so taken aback at my disdain for his favorite singer that he couldn't bring himself to get out of the car. We sat in the car in the movie theater parking lot while Danny continued to play different Tom songs in the hopes that I'd love the next one.

"What about this one?"

"Nope."

"Okay, but that one was great, right?"

"Not my taste."

Danny spent 133 minutes trying to change my mind.

It felt like Danny was invalidating every reason I gave for not liking Tom. Maybe this was because Danny spent two hours invalidating every reason I gave for not liking Tom.

With each changing of the track on the CD, I tried to ignore the growing dizziness that surrounded my listening brain. What Danny didn't understand was that this pushy method of trying to change my mind only succeeded in doing one thing—pushing my buttons. Specifically, the button labeled *Christine's Stubborn Streak*. Danny had no idea that he'd been messing with the rebel who shunned her required reading.

The book list that the high school English Department conjured up made me feel crazy confined—a lot like those tiny changing stalls at the Gap. When the school decreed that I must take my summer to read books off their list, I turned into a summer reading rebel. I banned my summer reading even in the face of possible detention, grounding, and never knowing if Madame Bovary ever cheered up. The next year I skipped the reading list all together. I still got an A.

I'm not proud of my behavior, but I'd happily have taken the failing grade and punishment that followed over not having a choice. When choices are blindly thrust upon me, oftentimes I'll just go and do the opposite out of principle. Or out of spite. Tom Waits never stood a chance.

Danny's car-time inquisition made me feel like I was fighting to keep my own individuality. I felt like he was trying to take me away from me—like he wanted me to trade in who I was for what he wanted. I wouldn't do it. If my stubborn streak could keep me from wondering if it really was *All Quiet on the Western Front* (Never read it. Still got an A.), who knows how long I could go on not liking Tom Waits. Weeks? Months? Years? All of the above.

My husband is of the opinion that I should revisit Tom. I should give Tom another chance based on the simple fact that he loves him so much. Danny wants me to love Tom because Danny loves Tom.

Armed with Tom Waits albums, Danny is forever on a crusade. Where once my husband openly tried to convince me that my opinion was askew, a new plan has taken shape. This new and improved tactic involves my husband trying to sneak Tom into my anti-Tom world.

Danny has taken to playing me unknown or new Tom Waits songs in the hopes that I'll not immediately recognize Tom's pseudo-casual tone. This way I might listen to Tom with an open mind and fresh ears. Danny believes that if I have *all* the facts, I will magically come to my senses and realize how I've misjudged his vocal hero.

Working under this assumption, my husband has started crafting "clever" little plans in order to trick me. The intended outcome of these slick schemes being my immediate adoration of Danny's all-time favorite.

The ruse begins with a CD being covertly placed in the player. The music starts, and I immediately hear a voice that I don't recognize. The tedious ballad drones on as I start trying to place the unknown songster, and this is about the time a new voice enters the mix. Ha! This song is a duet—with Tom Waits. I am so on to him.

Danny forever lives in a place of hope. In his world, a day will come when he will finally find the perfect Tom Waits song for me. When that day arrives, we will attend Tom Waits concerts hand in hand, and live happily ever after.

"Tom Waits is doing a concert tour."

"Uh huh . . ."

"I thought maybe I'd buy two tickets . . ."

"Oh? Who are you going to get to go with you?"

"Never mind."

I am so on to him.

I had hoped that after that initial crash course in everything Tom, Danny would realize that I didn't care for Mr. Waits. I feel like I've been pretty clear over the years regarding where I stand. But this hasn't stopped Danny from trying to convert me. And I see now that it never will.

After over ten years of his covertly playing Tom Waits songs, I understand that every time I reject Tom, I'm rejecting Danny. It's like I'm telling Danny I don't love him.

It's hard for Danny. He puts all of himself into what he loves. He has a hard time separating himself from his passions. Strangely, this strange paradox is what keeps me stubborn. Danny wants me to love Mr. Waits because he does. I want to be loved because I don't.

I've tried to explain to my husband that I can still love him even though he has horrible taste in music. Danny doesn't love everything I do. If he did, we'd have a more organized house, read poetry every afternoon, and watch *Xanadu* every Saturday night. I think he can love me and not love singing/roller-skating muses and Olivia Newton-John.

Like a long-playing record, we are stuck in a vicious circle: When my husband opens up a Tom CD, he is opening up his heart along with it—which my Stubborn Button unflinchingly rejects.

I still can't look at the cover of *A Tale of Two Cities* (Never read it. Still got an A.) without feeling dizzy with confinement. Danny, Tom Waits, and Charles Darnay all succeed in pushing my infamous Stubborn Button. However, I don't blame Charles and I don't blame Danny for triggering that little stubborn ball of tension. (All right, I do blame Danny a little.) But I know that is what gets my Stubborn Streak up and running, so for my husband I can try to stand still—or at least jog in place.

Maybe then Danny will finally understand that even though I don't love Tom Waits, I do love him. Maybe then my husband will hear me over that gravelly voice.

"It's a new song," Danny says hopefully. "Do you like it?"
This isn't *so* bad.
"It's a new song . . . by Tom Waits."
Oh no.
Should I tell him?

CHAPTER 22

Money Matters

How to share one income between two people

Ellen and Frank

"Honey, I'm going to buy the girls some Bubble Yum bubble gum today."

"Do they *need* bubble gum?"

Perhaps the Bubble Yum Conversation is a bit exaggerated. I don't really have to ask my husband's permission to buy some Bazooka. That would be stupid. I can troll under the car seats and between couch cushions in order to scrape up some unaccounted for extra change for the girls' bubble gum. My Husband the Exchequer doesn't need to know about the money I'm wasting on frivolous sweets.

The philosophies my husband and I have regarding the spending of money couldn't be more unalike. This rift is what turns me into a loose change scavenger. If asked to describe his financial planning system in one word, Frank would choose a prudent word like "frugal." If asked to describe Frank's planning system from *my* perspective, the word would be more like "hoarder."

My husband's "frugal" tendencies remind me of a squirrel—a busy summer squirrel terrified of the winter. My hardworking squirrel constantly stores nuts for the winter, but unlike a real squirrel, my husband would rather starve during the winter than dip into his hard-won supplies. I picture a tiny, furry squirrel version of my husband sitting in his little nest counting all his nuts, recounting them, and then sleeping on them just in case the wife squirrel decides she needs a midnight snack.

After nine years of living with Frank (and four looking for loose change), I know my husband well enough to understand that he just sees himself as "practical." Frank is trying to be the best provider he can be. Sadly, being the provider of the house tops being an equal financial partner.

Frank's monetary system revolves around the belief, "If the family doesn't really *need* it, we don't really *need* to buy it." I do understand this concept. This is why our two girls haven't been able to talk me into building a pony, puppy, and baby pig stable in the backyard—obviously something we don't *need*.

I agree with my husband—but only up to a point. My monetary system revolves around the belief, "What's money for if not to spend? (At least some of it.)" If Frank and I can safely afford something, what's wrong with buying some stuff we don't *need* every now and then? We may not *need* a couch, but they're fun to sit on.

It doesn't take a lot of money to live. I know this because I never had a lot of money—or any really. My family never starved, but we also never had any extra cash. I had one pair of shoes to last me from Christmas until Christmas. If I played outside too much and happened to wear a hole in the heel, there were no replacement shoes in my future. I just put on another pair of socks. (Santa doesn't do emergency shoes in the summer. He's a one-holiday kind of guy.)

Frank's family could afford all the shoes and socks he ever wanted. So I find it odd that he's the one of us concerned that another Great Depression is about to happen at any minute. My husband is forever saving and questioning me on how I choose to spend *our* money. I'm tired of defending my Bubble Yum buying.

I've been asking Frank to let me into his money man-cave for years now. (Ever since I quit my job to raise our two girls.) If my husband can let me into his heart, shouldn't he be able to let me into *our* finances? I assumed this kind of fifty-fifty monetary sharing would be a no-brainer, because that's what respectful married people do. They share. I like sharing our bed, our house, and our toothpaste, but so far I'm not so hot on sharing our cash. Even though Frank swears it's *ours*, it doesn't feel like it to me. It feels like Frank's.

Every Sunday I'm summoned to the kitchen. My hands begin sweating, and I try my best to remain calm. The conversation starts with Frank asking me about my weekly spending.

"So, did the kids really *need* those new Reebok Hightop shoes?"

"Yes, they really needed new shoes."

This is the part where I'm held accountable for every cent I've spent. Frank will then approve or disapprove of my purchases—all under the guise of saving money. The conversation continues with me defending said purchases, explaining to my breadwinning husband that someone does, in fact, need to buy the bread we eat. The whole thing feels wrong. I'm supposed to be a partner here, but what I feel like is an employee reporting to her boss.

I haven't yet reached the point where I dream about substituting rat poison for Skinny 'n Sweet in Frank's morning coffee. I know that whole plan didn't work out too well for Dolly Parton and Lily Tomlin in *9 to 5*. And Frank is not even as close to as bad as their boss was but I still don't want my husband to be the boss of me—or my finances—at all. I simply want a little trust and a little R-E-S-P-E-C-T.

Frank and I aren't totally on opposite sides of the accounting ledger. I agree with my husband that we need to know where all of our money is going. I think it's a good idea to keep track of it all. What I don't think is a good idea is grilling one's wife on why she chose to buy new shoes for her daughters or those patent leather ones for herself.

"And what about these sweaters?"

"Well Frank, it's getting cold outside . . ."

Frank has no idea what it takes financially to run a household. I've tried explaining to Frank that I only buy things we *need* (okay, I'm guilty of a few bubble gum indulgences and possibly a Twist 'n Curl Barbie for each girl), but I do take my stay-at-home-mom job very seriously. I know how to do my job.

Unlike other jobs, I get no sick days or paid vacation days. I get no benefits. (And no, that new "bonus" vacuum does not count as a "benefit." We can't live in a house coated in dog and cat hair—the kids' allergies would never be able to take it. See, I'm being money savvy, because a new vacuum is saving Frank millions in allergy shots and doctor bills.)

"And the grocery bill . . ."

" . . . is the grocery bill."

If only I could *Freaky Friday* Frank into my skin. Then he would really see how much it costs to run a house. He would see what a pair of shoes really costs and how much our groceries truly are. Still, maybe in order to save money, Freaky Friday Frank would resort to making the girls' clothes and mixing his own cleaning products.

It wouldn't be so bad if we could both have our own belief systems about money, but I'm forced to believe in Frank's. This imposed money "saving" system creates a massive amount of tension that honestly I'm not even sure my husband notices. If he does, he is such a devotee of how he is micromanaging *our* money that he doesn't care.

"Ellen, did the girls really *need* that Barbie?"

"Frank, sometimes a girl needs a new Barbie."

"Hmmm . . . I don't know that we can afford extra things like that."

And that's the problem. Since Frank doesn't tell me how much money we actually have, he does have a point—I don't know if we can afford it. I'm not exactly sure what my share is. I also don't know how much my husband is spending, and how much we have in our account. If we were equal business partners, this is something I'd know. Frank remains mute on both subjects. Then I see my husband spending *our* money on a tennis membership for himself and the occasional fancy business lunch, and that's when I figure we have a little extra cash for a Barbie doll here and there. (I mean, does he really *need* that membership?)

"Frank, I want a bigger part in our financial planning."

"Honey, you don't have to worry about it. I'm taking care of it."

Anytime I ask him to reveal our magic bank account number he says, "Don't worry. I'm taking care of it." I wasn't worried . . . until he started saying that.

On more than one occasion during our Sunday night "budgeting sessions" I've mentioned that I want to have a larger part in our financial planning. I explain that I think these sessions would go much more smoothly if I were more in the know. When I bring it up, he reminds me that he's "taking care of it." Am I supposed to feel more secure knowing my man is "taking care of it"? Is that what Frank thinks I want to hear? Instead of making me feel taken care of, it makes me feel untrustworthy.

So it's a definite possibility that, due to the stress of explaining why it's necessary to buy the kids new socks, along with Frank's manly need to keep *our* finances under wraps, my "why won't you share our finances with me?" tone has been far from pleasant.

My well-rehearsed monologues may have come out sounding more like a ranting Oscar the Grouch from *Sesame Street*. (Amy is on a *Sesame Street* kick.) Frank has the amazing talent of being able to tune out that particular tone. So, I shall be brave and take the less accusatory high road with my Husband the Exchequer.

"Honey, I'd really like to be more a part of all of our finances." Well done—calm, direct, honest, not a hint of a grouch in sight.

"I'm taking care of it."

Following Oscar's example, this would now be the point when I'm reduced to throwing old banana peels and breaking out into a little song about how much "I Love (throwing) Trash"—at my husband.

I have to disagree with Frank on this one—Frank isn't really "taking care of it."

Due to our non-system system, there are months when the checkbook doesn't balance. Those are the worst. There have been Sundays when I've forgotten something I've bought because I didn't write it down. (If I had something to write it down *in*—like a checkbook—that might help.) Or Frank didn't know that I was going to pick up a month's worth of dry cleaning, so he went ahead and paid for a fancy business lunch and voilà—overbudget.

If I had the rights and privileges afforded to any equal financial partner, I'd know how much Frank is spending and be better able to budget my share. When do I get my half of *our* funds? Is there some sort of form I can fill out to apply?

With Frank's *system*, I don't really get a share as much as a lecture on overspending. When I ask Frank what he's spent *our* money on, again he *reassures* me that he's "taking care of it." Is my husband spending his hard-earned wages on a secret Trans-Am? Is that why he won't he tell me?

Even though Frank does enjoy a good 1980s sports car as much as the next guy, more than having a midlife automobile crisis in his mid-thirties, I think Frank's inability to share is more about Frank wanting to be the man of the house. Frank feels the need to be in control of manly things like checking accounts and leaf blowers. (He'd probably sleep with the lawn mower if he could fit it in our bed.) I'm more than willing to let Frank have free rein over our leaf blower, lawn mower, or any other outdoor manly machinery he'd like. He can exert his manly prowess all over our front yard—go crazy! *Our* finances are not the same thing—even though Frank may see it that way.

It would seem I'm having a problem successfully explaining to my husband what the term "our money" really means. Thank goodness my crazy Bubble Yum buying rampages haven't put us into financial ruin, but all this miscommunication is beginning to ruin my trust—in us.

I've thought about being sneaky. I've thought about holding our checkbook hostage. Sadly, that's not an option that demonstrates a great deal of trust in *our* relationship. And that's what I want. I want us to be equal. I want Frank to trust me with everything. And I want to trust Frank.

"Honey," I started calmly, "you know, if we could come up with a system where I knew how much money we had in the account, we might not be short."

"Our system is fine. You just need to watch what you spend."

Wow.

The only thing Frank can hear is the sound of money leaving his checking account.

I get it now.

I can talk sweetly, I can summon my inner Oscar the Grouch, I can rant and rave until I am blue in the face—my husband is not going to hear me. Nothing I can say will ever change his manly monetary system. He knows himself to be right, and I am always going to be wrong.

Why can't he see his system isn't working? He's a smart guy. He's a brainy guy. If we had a better shared system, these Sunday night inquisitions would be a thing of the past. There would be no more questions, no more overspending, and in its place would be not only a more balanced checkbook, but a more balanced relationship.

I've tried my best to be the solution. I've tried every way I can think of to get through to his manly psyche. I bet if I were a guy, he'd listen to me. And that's when it hit me—nothing I can say will change his mind. But what about another guy? What if something someone else says could influence him? Could that work? If I can't *be* the solution in our relationship, what would happen if I brought a solution *into* our relationship?

I planned my moment carefully. I'd ask him after he returned home from winning a tennis match . . .

"Honey, you know, sometimes we're short of cash. I just thought that if we talked to Doug about it, maybe he could give us some help."

I saw him process. I saw the little smile that flashed across his face.

"That's not a bad idea," Frank began. "He could help with a budget."

That last sentence was directed at me. I got the sarcastic hint. He truly believed I needed to stop overspending, while I truly believed I had just saved our marriage—and our bank account.

Many times over the years, our accountant Doug has come through for us. Frank respects his learned opinion. Maybe he feels more comfortable listening to Doug because Doug has the diploma above his desk and I do not. Or because Doug has a penis and I do not. (I may have balls, but that's not the same thing.) Whatever the reason, Frank trusts Doug.

I know I'm not irresponsible with money. I'm just not Frank. I know it's our system that is flawed. I'm convinced that a smart man like Doug will quickly see that we need to change our process. I'm hoping that my husband will hear him.

Talking to Doug turned out to be the best investment we ever made.

Doug informed my husband that I needed to be an equal part of our financial planning. (I could've told Frank that. In fact I did.) Doug also explained that I would need my own checking account, and in it would be put the money that I needed to run the household.

I couldn't tell if Frank was bothered by these suggestions or not, but I guess his ego wasn't too bruised, because we left Doug's and promptly opened my own checking account.

I was a little shocked that Frank took Doug's advice so quickly. I expected Oscar the Grouch would have to raise his ugly head at least once more. I thought there'd be a long discussion in the car about our "perfect" system, but there was not. There was only a little black checkbook sitting happily in my purse. Somewhere in his deep dark manly money mancave Frank was willing to trust me. We were finally on our way to a truly equal financial partnership—and a more equal marriage.

Now I'll always have enough money to buy bubble gum . . . and sometimes I'll even share a piece with my husband.

CHAPTER 23

For Better or for Worst

How to work through the tough times

Chloe and Malcolm

It's what he's not saying that's scaring me.

I tell myself it's such a little thing. I remind myself that everything is normal—even though I don't feel that way. How can one tiny phrase left unuttered punch such a huge hole in me? Something is not right. Malcolm has stopped asking me about my day. What have I done wrong?

"Mal, are you all right?"

"I'm fine."

I hate to accuse someone of lying, but Malcolm is definitely not telling me the truth. He may have succeeded in convincing himself he's fine, but it's clear to me that he's anything but.

The first couple of times Mal forgot to ask me about my day, I ignored it. So what if he forgot to ask me about me? I don't have to tell Mal about my day to prove I had one. He probably has a lot on his mind with his new job.

It took me a full week to realize what I already knew—the absence of that simple question was a symptom of something greater.

My normally confident man has gone from being excited about life, to walking around like a dejected Peanuts character. His head hangs low, and his eyes are dull and lost in thought. There's a space growing between us, and I feel like all that space may suffocate me. I must have said something to ruffle his feathers. I wonder what it was.

I've always trusted Malcolm to tell me the truth, because he always has—a welcome change from friends who didn't. Sure, I was in junior high. Sure, that was a while ago. Sure, twelve-year-olds are not always an entirely reliable source of relationship information (or fashion advice), but I had learned a valuable lesson: I rub people the wrong way without having a clue what I did.

My junior high experience was like walking into a *Twilight* convention only to shout innocently that *Buffy the Vampire Slayer* is the best vampire series of all time. (Not the best entrance in the world of vampires.) Everyone but me knew I had made the most inappropriate of statements, but somehow I missed the vampire memo. (Must have come during the day.)

My twelve-year-old friends' frosty silence spoke volumes. I was left trying to figure out what I'd done or said that was so wrong. There was an awkwardness between me and my friends that never really abated, and all I wanted to do was fix whatever I had done. It's a real challenge trying to put together a puzzle without the pieces. I trusted my friends to tell me the truth about me—and they never did. But Malcolm always does.

The quiet that I'm feeling from Malcolm is eerily similar to the one in those early teen years. It's awkward and empty. I feel deserted by my best friend just for being myself. I can't let this go unfixed. At least this time I know to keep my vampire-loving preferences to myself, but I thought I was safe with Malcolm. We both love *Buffy*.

I must have done *something*.

Thus far our emotional life together has been smooth. We've had misunderstandings, but we've always talked them through. This is one of the many things I trust about us. The possibility that he might stop talking never entered my mind.

"Mal, are you sure you don't want to talk . . . about *your* day?"

"I'm fine."

The absence of his daily question overwhelms me. I keep telling myself to let it go. He still holds my hand. He still tells me he loves me. But I never want to be faulted for missing the warning signs.

There's always foreshadowing. Any good writer knows this. I've always wondered why such savvy literary heroines miss the obvious signals. Most of these leading ladies are bright women who are somehow totally unaware of the tragic fate that awaits them.

If they'd read the signs (or the CliffsNotes), Cleopatra and Juliet would have lived happy lives with their loves, and Bella would have stayed human instead of becoming a childbearing vampire. I'm not ignoring this sign.

Where once lounged interested chatter now sits a silence. This silence hangs in the room long after my Malcolm has left it. My overactive imagination has decided to fill this uncomfortable space with something even scarier than the quiet itself—thoughts. Chaotic thoughts run through my head like starving zombies chasing after their next human snack.

Is it me? He always asks me about my day. That's what we do. I regale him with long tales of what happened today while he listens. Why has he stopped asking? Are my stories that boring?

Occasionally, I get snippets of conversation from him.

"Mal, how was work?"

"Not good."

"Are you all right?"

"I'm fine."

Those lively conversations have not been a whole lot of help.

Since Mal is remaining curiously silent on the subjects of his feelings and my day, I've deemed it prudent to figure out how he's feeling for him. So far this is not working too well—which is weird because, more often than not, I can tell when Mal is bothered before he can tell he's bothered. Mal leaves me subtle conversational clues that only I can decipher.

"Chloe, I feel weird."

"What did you do today?"

"Work was crazy. I never stopped . . ."

"Did you stop to eat?"

"No."

"Mal, you're hungry."

I wish this time it were that simple. This time around I can't get a handle on it.

If Malcolm isn't talking *to* me, then maybe what he's pondering so silently is *about* me. It must be. I must have done something to cause such a growing silence. Why won't he tell me? What if he can't tell me? What if is he's afraid of hurting my feelings? What if he will hurt my feelings? What if it's me?

"Mal, are you all right?"

"I'm fine."

His stoic silence gives my zombie thoughts crazy-fast superpower strength. They are unstoppable.

Is it me? It must be me. I ate all the chocolate ice cream. I didn't mean to. I just looked down and it was gone. Go out now and buy more ice cream. Why won't he talk to me? Oh no. Don't tell him you ate all the vanilla too.

It must be me.

"Mal, I can tell something is bothering you."

"I'm fine."

More than one "I'm fine" in a day adds up to not fine at all.

My feminine logic tells me that if I ask enough, the love of my life will eventually open up and confide in me. But in this particular situation, my female wisdom needs to take the day off and go get a pedicure, because this poking way of questioning never seems to work the way I envision.

I try to stop asking the same question over and over again, but something like my brain takes control of my mouth, and I ask again . . . and again . . . and maybe just one last time will do the trick. I can't stand it. I need to find out what I've done. Why won't he tell me?

"Mal, are you sure you don't want to talk?"

"I'm fine. Please stop asking me, Chloe."

Everything is not fine.

He used my name.

I'm in trouble.

When my name curtly ends our conversation, I know Malcolm is done—with me. I can hear it in his tone. I feel like I've been shoved on the playground. So, I do what any nice, well-adjusted kid pushed in the sandbox would do—push back.

"Do *NOT* talk to me like that—ever."

"Chloe, what did I say?"

Shoving back harder, I add, "It's not what you said. It's *HOW* you said it."

I wonder if Antony and Cleopatra ever had such astute exchanges?

Sometimes one or both of us walk off in a righteous huff. Other times the conversation quickly escalates, and we end up arguing about lofty subjects like who last made the bed. I find that bed making is never a good basis for a deep argument. (Because it's always Malcolm's turn.)

I'm not sure which is worse, the quiet or the arguing. Both make me feel lousy. Both magnify the unsolvable problem that we're having. I never thought I'd get the twelve-year-old silent-ish treatment from the love of my life. What if suddenly he turns on me like they did?

I can't remember another time in our life together as a couple that's been this hard to navigate. Arguing about bed linens isn't something either of us cares about much. Another huge flashing sign that all is not well in the state of us.

When I try my hardest to give Malcolm his space, I panic. The space in the quiet overtakes any sort of rational thought. I try to ignore it, but the more I try to ignore it, the more I ask. The more I ask, the more Mal retreats. If he'd talk to me about what was going on, then I'd leave him alone. It's simple. How many times do I have to ask before he shares?

My thoughts are getting too good at making up awful scenarios containing varying versions of a cranky Malcolm who never snaps out of it.

The movie in my mind plays clips of a future where I have forever lost the man I fell in love with to days of fighting and nights of unmade beds. How do I get to the truth versus what *might* be happening?

My usual open and communicative Malcolm has taken a vacation. I want to remind him that as his partner I'm allowed certain vacation privileges (like going with him), but this holiday, I have no choice but to stay behind. Mal has taken a trip to a place that I can't easily follow—into his head.

It seems to me he's not having a really good time on this trip. Instead of sunscreen, his face is covered in pensiveness. Maybe the vacation waiters keep forgetting his fruity umbrella drink?

It must be me.

Waiting around for Mal to tell me what's going on and suffering through his moody silences are not the way I want to spend the evenings with the man I love. Am I just supposed to stop asking simply because Malcolm doesn't want to talk?

I found a quiet moment to ask, "What's going on?"

"Work," was his in-depth response.

"What are you working on?"

"Work stuff."

This was going well.

"Can I help with anything?"

"I'm fine."

And there it was again. I know he's not. We both know he's not. Again I wanted to keep pressing him. I wanted to dig his feelings out of his chest to find out what I'd done—why he wasn't talking. My zombie thoughts considered eating his brain so maybe then I'd know all he knew, but that seemed a little much. Zombie thoughts are nothing if not inventive—and slightly gross.

Taking a step out of my own pushy needs, I looked at Mal. He was so stressed out and sad.

"You know," I started, "if your job is that bad, you could just quit."

Malcolm looked at me with eyes alive and alert.

"What did you say?"

Oh no.

Had I done it again? Had I inserted my foot straight into my mouth without even knowing?

I thought about changing the sentence to something like, "If your job is that bad, you could just *spit*," but that rhyme wasn't going to cut it. (It was the best I could do in a millisecond.) It was already out there, so I could do nothing but repeat, "You could just quit and get another job."

Malcolm looked down and said, "I really hate it there . . ."

I'd said the right thing. I'd broken through.

Before Malcolm stopped asking me about my day, he mentioned that he wasn't all that happy at work. Mal's crankiness had been so severe, and his mentioning of work had been so blasé, that I had just assumed that I'd been the problem.

Mal finally opened up and told me that his crappy boss was setting him up for failure with a work contest. If he didn't win, he'd lose his job. It was a horrible position to be put in, especially since we had moved here three months ago so Mal could go to work at this dream job. His dream job was a nightmare. Why hadn't he told me all this?

"Why didn't you tell me all this?"

"Because, I'm fine."

And that was the sign for which I'd been waiting.

It wasn't me.

In an instant I got it. I did know Malcolm. I'd bet him a *Buffy* box set of DVDs that if he'd admitted to me how unhappy he'd been these past few weeks, he would've had to admit it to himself. That's why he was so cranky—he couldn't.

It wasn't me.

"I'm so sorry that it's been so hard. Is there anything I can do to help?"

Malcolm thought for minute, "I can't think when you keep asking me what's wrong. I need time . . ."

Oh.

That's not exactly what I'd meant. I was thinking more along the lines of going out to get a pizza and a couple of beers.

It comes down to whether or not I trust Malcolm to tell me what's bothering him. It's hard when I've always known or he's always told me. It's even worse when deranged zombies incessantly terrorize my brain.

So, I'm just expected to trust him? I'm supposed to walk around in silence waiting for him to talk when he's good and ready? What if he's never ready? What if we stay there forever?

Enough.

I can try. For Malcolm, I can try.

"All right. I can do that."

Malcolm's face relaxed. The quiet that had been was filled with something gentler. This was better.

"When you're ready," I waited for him to hear me, "I'd like to talk about what's been going on."

And we did.

The two of us finally started having honest conversations about his job *and* how to manage the hard times in our relationship. We may not be in a perfect place, but thank goodness there's talking. We're getting better at conquering the quiet. And on the days we aren't, on the days it creeps back into our lives, I let it. I may not be able to fix every bump in our relationship because (I'm learning) some things aren't mine to fix.

We're really talking about what our relationship means and where we want it to go. Our late-night talks in an unmade bed are helping us understand the intricacies of us. This includes learning to give my Mal his space and Mal trying not to take his cranky out on me. We're getting better at being together.

I don't know yet how to live comfortably in the awkward quiet (mainly because it's awkward), but Mal needs that strange silence to process his thoughts—I'm trying to give it to him, trusting that when he's ready he will *want* to talk to me. So, I'm doing my best to vanquish my pushy, anxious zombie thoughts. It's time to give my pushiness a little shove back—out of my love life.

Luckily, this avid reader has read her signs. For example, I know that for us when things appear to be at their worst—they'll get better. And that's a really, really good sign.

CHAPTER 24

The Puppy Gene Syndrome

How to bring out the puppy love in your husband

Tonilyn and Michael

I don't have a problem child. I have a problem dog. To Percy, the word "no" does in fact mean "yes," and the command "stay" translates as "RUN! FAST!" Percy is smart. Percy is special. Percy has the amazing ability to push every one of my husband's buttons, and it's my fault.

I have a rare genetic disorder—Puppy Gene Syndrome. PGS affects all the women in my family. Whenever a puppy is present, this affliction renders us incapable of rational thought. PGS works like this: We see a puppy. We want it. A cure has yet to be discovered.

In my family the phrase, "We're going to *look* at puppies," translates as "We are going to go bring *home* a puppy." There were many afternoons, when my father arrived at the house to find a fluffy surprise with a long tongue and floppy ears waiting in the living room. (And I'm not talking about my little sister.) What could my dad say to three giddy girls and a happy puppy at his feet?

One peculiar side effect of this syndrome is its inexplicable ability to render the alpha male of a family group completely powerless:

"What do you think?!?" my PGS raged. "Do you like him?"

"Well," Michael paused, "I'm not going to say no . . ."

That was all I needed. Percy was ours. Like my father years before, my husband, the "alpha male," found himself at home with a sweet and happy new puppy.

Puppies have a lot of energy. Border collie puppies have even more energy. As far as Percy was concerned, one would think we had substituted Red Bull for his water and given him earplugs to wear.

"Are you sure he's not deaf?" my sister asked after watching Percy one afternoon. I was sure.

Percy had the uncanny ability to completely ignore you. He gave you absolutely no sign that he'd heard a word you said. A person could shout, whistle, clap, or fire off small explosives and still nothing would register behind those happy brown eyes. It was a constant barrage of water bowls being purposely tipped over, peeing in the house, energetic bursts that lasted two hours, scraped hardwood floors, loud barking, and cat chasing. Percy had a full schedule.

Percy was proving himself a slow learner, and the more often he needed to be corrected, the more my husband became really annoyed. The more Percy ignored my husband's commands, the more irritated Michael became. The more Michael became irritated, the more his countenance contorted, and it was then that I could feel it. It was then that I could hear it. Michael's exasperated tone began to take on a quality I had never heard before. I could hear Percy's correction tempered with anger.

My husband doesn't get angry. (Unless he's watching his losing Dallas Cowboys playing the Washington Redskins.) Even our fights are not really *fights*. We are more very serious talkers. So for Michael to be so mad with our new puppy was more than unsettling to me. It was horrible.

In those moments, I felt like I didn't know my husband at all. It was like I was watching him turn from the sensitive Anakin Skywalker into the menacing Darth Vader right before my eyes. I was not about to create more conflict by getting my lightsaber out of the garage in order to fight him. I was left feeling empty and powerless—powerless to help my husband and powerless to help my puppy.

I really couldn't shake this heavy feeling that I was completely responsible for creating this situation. Ultimately, it had been my want that had brought Percy into our lives. PGS had been a fun and cute quirk as a child, but as an adult, this endearing "condition" had backfired something awful. I began to worry that I had pushed Michael too hard into getting a second dog. I feared that I had gently steamrolled my husband into a responsibility for which he wasn't ready.

In my family, PGS had always been viewed as a lovable syndrome. This condition had never been perceived as a negative—until now. Wanting to help both man and beast, I set about trying to find ways to ease the tension between the two.

First, I tried to take on most of the puppy work. I hoped that in my shouldering more of the daily responsibilities, Michael would feel less tense and therefore less frustrated. I also began training more with Percy—working on all those commands that might give Michael a moment of peace. However, these attempts didn't seem to ease the aggravation my husband still felt whenever Percy darted frantically around the room. Michael's frustration was clearly not abating, and Percy was not showing any signs of improvement.

I was running out of ideas.

I wondered how I was able to keep my cool through Percy's wild antics and not rise to that angry place. Sure, sometimes I felt irked as I looked at the mess Mr. Percy had lovingly left for me. But that moment of frustrated disbelief disappeared once I gazed into those innocent, trusting puppy eyes. I couldn't manage an ounce of anger.

It didn't matter how naughty Percy had been. I loved him anyway. I loved his water bowl tipping and constant running. I loved everything about him. Percy was just a puppy, and that's what puppies do—wreak havoc. Perhaps this realization could help mend the broken invisible fence, and we could all start anew. Perhaps I could bring some peace back into the household that my PGS had disrupted.

When I first brought up the idea of getting a second dog, my husband had been honest in expressing his concerns. Michael had confessed that since he hadn't come from a multi-pet household, the idea of being responsible for two dogs intimidated him.

As a married couple, Michael and I had agreed to listen to and respect the other's feelings and fears. Had I listened? Had I truly pushed him too hard? What could be done now, short of sending Percy packing?

"Do you love Percy?" I asked Michael on one of our pack walks.

"Of course, I do," Michael quickly answered. "I just don't love that he goes crazy all the time," he added after a beat.

"Well," I paused, "maybe if you try to see Percy with that love first, then the frustrating things he does won't seem so frustrating."

Michael was quiet all the way home.

That love had been the missing element in Michael and Percy's relationship.

It was a slow change, but I began to notice a difference in Michael with our puppy. The more my husband began to accept Percy, the calmer Percy became. The more my husband corrected him with a firm tone filled with love, the more Percy began to mind.

It was an amazing transformation to witness on both their parts. And that's when Percy and Michael started becoming the best of friends.

It seems we may have found that long-awaited cure for my PGS—cute, crazy Percy has done the trick. It's taken a lot of effort, a lot of time, and a whole lot of love, but Michael and I have finally found our footing with our crazy pup.

Michael and I have also found a new balance in our relationship, because let's be honest—Percy wasn't the only one in the house who hadn't been totally listening.

→HUSBAND RAISING 101←

It's rarely the over-the-top, glamorous, romantic stunts that are important. It's the daily and/or weekly practice of putting your relationship first that means the most.

—CHLOE on how to bring out the love in her marriage

In any good drama, it's the misunderstandings that create conflict. And in any good marriage, the same holds true. Marital misunderstandings happen in even the most loving of relationships, and it's in these moments of conflict that "bringing out the love" helps open communication to resolve the issues quickly so that a deep emotional bond will have room to grow.

In each situation these wives inspired their husbands to meet them in a comfortable middle ground, even when the tough issue seemed to have no possible resolution. Our leading ladies tried their best to honor their partners' point of view even when it conflicted with their own (or when they were simply dead wrong). This helped them walk that tricky line of compromise while holding on to their own individuality—all the while keeping themselves, and their good taste in music, intact.

SKILL BUILDING COVERED IN PART III

- ☐ How to bake a vanilla cake
- ☐ How to keep a focused and loving connection during busy times
- ☐ How to share money in a marriage
- ☐ How to stay true to yourself when faced with bad music choices
- ☐ How to reignite a loving bond in a stale marriage
- ☐ How to feel important when being brushed aside
- ☐ How and when it's appropriate to wear your cheerleading uniform

PART IV

RAISING 'EM RIGHT

Finding Balance

CHAPTER 25

All Right to Cry

Finding your true self

Lily and Gus

EXT. OCEAN/NIGHT

Rose kisses Jack's hand as she watches him sink into the dark of the ocean.

Music swells

ROSE:

(Crying, to Jack)

I'll never let go, Jack. I promise.

I can let go.

I promise.

My husband is a big softy—crying at the mere mention of certain greeting card commercials. Unlike other rough-and-tumble men, Gus is definitely in touch with his feminine side. (Too bad this feminine side doesn't do windows.) I love him for his sensitive soul. However, Gus's decidedly sensitive side makes me feel less than girly.

I thought I was supposed to be the one who gushed over coffee commercials filled with giddy dancing snowmen? Where's my graceful, ladylike heart? Gus promises me that my thick skin is nothing to cry about. He doesn't have to worry—I won't. My husband will cry enough for the both of us.

I used to think I was a fairly normal genteel girl. It never occurred to me that my skin might be a little thicker than most. Really, I never noticed any overt signs. I like pink and Hello Kitty just as much as the next girl. (I like pink anyway.) I am keenly aware that *Casablanca* is not a comedy. I figured I was okay.

Then I met Gus. His lovely delicate heart makes me look like the Child Catcher from *Chitty Chitty Bang Bang*. "There are children here somewhere. I can smell them." Cue the maniacal laugh and fiendish hand-ringing. I noticed our difference right from the start. The titanic signs were hard to miss.

I have no heart.

That's what I was thinking as I watched *Titanic* sink and Rose release Jack's lifeless hand into the frigid sea. I heard a symphony of handbags being unzipped. I looked around the movie theater only to see the entire female movie-going population searching for a hankie.

Moments after The Great Pocketbook Rustling of '97, I saw an ocean of white tissues silhouetted against the dark of the movie screen. It was eerie. I turned to my left, and there sat my future husband who was barely able to breathe. His chest was convulsing in huge sobs. I was amazed that man-sized tears were running down Gus' face like I run to get my morning doughnut. And then there I was—eyes dry.

I felt terrible that my handsome date was a mess of tears, and all I could think was "Can I get more Twizzlers?" Lovely. Gus was going to think I was a heartless swine. At least I got some free popcorn.

I slumped lower in my seat. Perhaps I could fake some tears? I'm an actor. Okay, maybe I could just rub salt from the popcorn in my eyes?

Out of the corner of my dry left eye, I could see Gus. He was inconsolable. I would have offered him a tissue—if I had one. What is wrong with me? In the background I heard Celine belting about how her heart would go on, and I just wished I had one. It was clear. Gus was the most beautifully sensitive man on the planet, while I was the only woman on this planet who did not cry at the end of *Titanic*. The only woman. On this planet. What is wrong with me?

I have no heart.

Luckily, Gus and I don't spend every available second watching *Titanic*, *Old Yeller*, and *Miss Congeniality*. Even my apparent nerves of steel couldn't handle that. My husband is so sensitive, he won't even watch certain movies. They are just too sad. (So French films are always out.) It's not that he wants to project a paragon of manly strength for all to marvel at, he simply doesn't want to feel sad. Even some books can be too much for his delicate nature.

"I finished it! I finished *The Prince of Tides*!" Gus announced.

"*Yay!* Didn't you love it? And how about that last page . . ."

"I didn't read the last page."

"Huh?"

"It was going to be too sad. I didn't want to say goodbye to Dr. Lowenstein."

Oh.

I read the last page first. Apparently, I can bear to say goodbye to Dr. Lowenstein before I've even met her.

My inability to cry at the latest holiday commercial never really bothered me—until I met Gus. It was then I started wondering if something was wrong with me. Mostly, because I wondered if my non-girly nature bothered my more girly husband. Generally, my husband is quick to inform me of my other inadequacies. Horrible things like leaving the coffee scoop in the coffee grounds the wrong way. If the handle isn't reaching out of the coffee grounds for the next person to grab (which is usually Gus), he is less than pleased.

"Lily, it's just so easy to shove the bowl end of the scoop in first. Please, could you try?"

Gus has never said, "Lily, it's just so easy to cry at *Pete's Dragon*. Please, could you try?"

There have been many a demonstration and many a discussion about the coffee scoop. There has never once been a discussion about my dry eyes. Sometimes, I just feel weird being less emotional than my husband.

I'm the girl. I'm the one who is supposed to carry tiny packages of tissues in her purse and extra mascara just in case mine runs while watching the puppies play in the park. Gus is supposed to be the strong, bristly man who remains impassive when faced with a new romantic comedy on TBS. How did our roles become so reversed?

Gus' deep sensitivity continues to glaringly point out my great lack of it. Gus sweetly swears that he loves me despite my deficiency, so maybe he's telling the truth. Maybe it doesn't bother him. Maybe he can sense that underneath it all, I am emotional. I have cried in my lifetime. I cried when I graduated high school. True, they were tears of joy, but it was the end of a significant era, and I sensed that.

I cried at our wedding.

Gus cried right out of the gate, but as soon as we started our vows, I felt my body tighten and I could feel a pressure in my chest. (And not just because my dress was tight.) Listening to Gus say our vows while watching the happy tears fall down his cheeks was more than my tiny heart could handle. I felt my usually dry eyes become wet.

I may not cry at sappy commercials or every Disney movie, but I do cry. I cry when it counts. Standing at the altar, my husband-to-be and I were crying—together.

Some people might label my husband a sap and move on. Some people might say I'm unsentimental and move on. It doesn't matter. I know who my husband is, and I love my big softie. My husband knows who I am, and thank goodness he loves his thick-skinned wife.

Just as my husband thoughtfully provides me with extra Twizzlers at movies, I'll proudly hold my husband's hand and lovingly provide a hankie while he weeps his way through *Modern Family*. I'm happy to support him in his sensitive moments—just as he supports me during my lack of them. Gus and I may have swapped roles, but I see that there's beauty in the difference.

It is all right to cry—and sometimes it's all right not to too.

CHAPTER 26

Write All Along

Finding belief in yourself and in your husband

Chloe and Malcolm

There's one question that continually stumps me. Before I get the chance to give my answer, my mouth flies open, happy to contradict my brain. While the brain in my head shouts, "No! That's not what I wanted to say," a jumble of half-truths stumble out of my mouth like a sixteen-month-old child trying to run. This is when my husband speaks for me.

"She's a writer," he answers confidently, while I stand there trying to look like one.

How does one stand when one is a writer? Do my uni-ball pens need to be visible at all times? Should I be carrying many leather-bound notebooks to make it official? I'm just not sure what's considered proper author etiquette. Without published proof, I feel like a poser telling people I'm a writer merely based on the fact that I write.

"So, what do you do?"

"Well . . .I . . . er . . . I'm a writer."

My answer already has me sounding like a person who can't manage a few coherent words, let alone pen a few lines of dialogue.

While the first question makes me feel like a faker, I know my answer to the next question is only going to make me feel like an idiot.

"You're a writer. What have you written?"

"Well . . . I . . . eh . . . nothing."

The wannabe writer is revealed. Other than the grocery list I wrote this morning, I haven't written anything of import.

Once I become a *published* writer, then clearly I'll always carry around copies of my work–taped to my face. People won't even have to ask me what I do when that happens. They'll just know because the evidence will be hard to miss–taped to my face.

I dream of the day when I'll have tangible proof so others, besides my husband and my dog, will know I'm a writer. When that happens, I won't feel like such a fraud. Oddly, Malcolm doesn't seem to think it matters.

"Chloe, why don't you just tell people you're a writer?"

"Because I haven't published anything."

"*Yet* . . . you haven't *yet*. And you are a writer. You *write*."

I thought about responding to the "What do you do?" question by saying I *want* to be a writer. But that sounds like a little kid saying that she'd like to be a princess or a vampire slayer. I suppose being a princess isn't totally impossible, but being a vampire slayer might be a little more challenging–vampires are hard to track down.

My non-writing day job is my salary, so when strangers ask, "What do you do?" I respond with the more practical answer, even though my heart sinks a little every time. I clumsily mutter something about my 9 to 5 job and leave out the writing part. My day job is what I *do*. Writing is what I *want* to do. People don't generally go around asking, "What do you *want* to do?"

I've always wanted to be a writer. That is if *always* counts as since I was twenty-one years old. Too bad I didn't hear my calling until the very end of my last semester of senior year.

My major in environmental studies had nothing to do with writing unless you count writing essays about the interdisciplinary analysis of ecological systems in Japan as such. I had a huge end-of-the-year project due, and instead of going the normal long boring essay route, my end-of-the-year project started out as a picture book, which graduated into a full-blown children's novel.

I loved working on that project, and that was my first hint that writing might just be for me. I was nervous to tell Malcolm, since I was considering changing my entire life plan, but I shouldn't have been.

When I announced to him that I thought I wanted to be a writer, he never flinched. He didn't look at me like I was a loon or lecture me on picking a career in my chosen field. Mal was instantly supportive.

I'm not sure what I expected Malcolm to do. Yell at me and force me into a tedious life of air and soil analysis? I was changing the direction of our lives, yet he never seemed upset that I was choosing a job that might not provide us with financial security. It's almost like he actually thought I'd be a good writer or like he was proud of me for taking a chance and doing what I truly wanted to do or something.

I should be just as proud of my choice as my husband is. It should be me. I should be able to tell people what I do without embarrassment. It would be nice to be as supportive of myself as he is. But maybe Mal's support is about something else? I supported him all through graduate school, so maybe it's more like returning the favor?

While Mal was buried in grad school studies, I was buried in mounds of ice cream. My day job consisted of scooping over thirty-one flavors, and I was not a fan—of the job. I am a fan of ice cream. During that time, I could have thought of over thirty-one more fun ways of spending my time (possibly eating ice cream instead of scooping it), but as much as that job wasn't for me, I didn't mind. It wasn't permanent, and I knew it needed to be done for the good of us. I was happy to wield my scoop if it helped Mal.

I felt like if the situation were reversed Mal would do the same thing for me—and now it is and now he is. So why am I the first one to swiftly edit my lifelong ambition out of a conversation, while Malcolm is the first one to proudly put it in? How can my husband see me as a writer when I can't? I'm the one sitting at the desk writing. (He's the one sitting at the desk playing video games.) I want to tell people I'm a writer. I just don't believe I am one.

It's so hard for me to self-identify without proof of who I am. I have a paycheck that proves I have a job. I have a diploma that says I graduated from college. I have a husband that proves I have a husband. I wish someone could write me a diploma, or a notarized letter, or give me a little certificate so that I could prove to people I'm a writer. In this case, I don't think a note from my mother will suffice.

Maybe a note from the government will.

"Mal, you can't fill out our tax form that way!"

He squinted, pursed his lips and said, "This is asking for your occupation, and you are a writer."

Malcolm is going to jail.

Tall men in black suits will show up at our door demanding to see Malcolm. These men with skinny ties will grab Mal by the arm and force him out of our apartment. My husband will be lost to me forever. I will have successfully orchestrated his doom.

Mal is trying to make a point. But I can't let him. I'm not a writer.

"Mal, seriously . . . you can't write 'writer' there. I'm not a writer."

"You write. You are a writer."

Mal is not going to budge. I can tell by his expression and the permanent ink he is using to fill in the blank space labeled "occupation."

Staring at the word "writer" in the space marked "occupation" left me dumbfounded. It looked false. It looked weird. It felt good.

I never thought seeing my name next to the word "writer" would be such a satisfying thing. Instead of wanting to run to the nearest store and buy some Wite-Out, I wanted to frame it.

Through all the hesitancy and the misgivings, I am proud of what I want to be. I am proud of what I am—a writer.

Maybe I don't have to have tomes of published works sitting in the backseat of my car or my latest published article (taped to my face) to prove I'm a writer. Proof or no proof, no one is going to believe I am a writer until I do. This might just be the best place to start.

Mal is right, I am writing even if I'm not earning. The thing that makes me a writer is writing. The government should know what I plan on doing with the rest of my life, and I should start owning it—especially if they are going to take my money *when* I start making it.

CHAPTER 27

The Social Butterfly

Finding the support you need

Tonilyn and Michael

I can make out the top of my husband's head from thirty feet away.

Being a foot taller than the average partygoer does make him easier to spot in a crowd. If Michael decides to sit down amidst the throng, I also have a highly successful backup method of finding him—his laugh. His laugh cuts through the ambient noise of a crowd like a Whitesnake song at a bowling alley.

I can always find the most popular kid at the party, my husband, from my vantage point in the most unpopular spot of the party—the corner. I wonder if we'll ever meet in the middle . . . or even at the front door?

As the shyest kid at the party, I've become adept at picking out the best corner. Corners are safe. Corners are quiet. Corners are dark. I like corners. The only true downside is the lack of lighting they provide. Corners are generally too dark for me to catch up on my reading. I've thought about bringing an audiobook, but I doubt I'd be able to hear it over the din. Sadly, I'm never as productive as I'd like to be at a party.

Why do I lurk in shadowy corners trying to read? I like to avoid the one thing that is required while attending a party—talking. Talking isn't so much my bag. It's my husband's.

Michael is a master of the art of the Small Talk. I am a master of the art of the Smile and Nod. Michael is a beautiful social butterfly. I'm a clumsy moth attracted to the flame of the television in my living room—and dark party corners. Michael can visit comfortably for hours—maybe even days. I can converse awkwardly for seventeen minutes and twenty-four seconds. After I've exhausted my main go-to topics—the weather and a person's health—I begin scoping out the best corner.

There are only so many times I can discuss the crazy high-pressure system coming in from the north before I want to go home and watch *American Pickers*. I have married my complete and total social opposite.

I'll admit it, I don't flit well at parties. I stumble and trip on the simplest of greetings and phrases. I'm awkwardly repetitive. I'm awkwardly repetitive. Sometimes the only solution is to stuff my mouth full of homemade brownies from the dessert table so that I might have an excuse to stop talking (and eat brownies).

The first real parties I went to were in college. I don't think my tween-age Madonna lip-sync birthday parties count, and annual Fourth of July lawn parties with my parents definitely don't count. The latter I could bring a book to without being classified as too much of a nerd. I quickly discovered that one does not bring a book to a college party. One brings a bottle of Night Train or several bottles of Bartles & Jaymes berry wine coolers. Books and college don't mix. Live and learn.

Since bringing a book and doing some light reading at a college kegger were out of the question, I decided to bring something even better—a boyfriend! My boyfriend could be my buffer! It was genius. I wouldn't have to do any talking as long as we stuck together. My gregarious boyfriend could be my wingman, and since we've all learned the valuable lesson from Maverick, "You never leave your wingman!" I knew I'd be safe.

There was a gentle but forcefully whispered reminder from me at the beginning of each party that went something like "*Do not leave me alone!*" With those explicit instructions even a child could grasp, how could my boyfriend and I not have a fabulous time watching drunk people make out and then fall down?

Maybe Deee-Lite was playing too loudly in the background, because my boyfriend never heard the most important word in my request—*not*. It's like I said, "*Do leave me alone.*"

This was when I learned about dark corners, stuffing my mouth full of dessert table brownies, and consequently what the "Freshman 15" meant.

Over the years, my party-going script has not changed by much. This time around I carry a cell phone and a husband. While corners are not conducive to book reading, they are perfect for iPhone gaming. I've found this to be a wonderful method for fooling groups of people into thinking that I'm very busy and important in my own little corner. However, this tactic does not fool my husband.

When I start snaking my way to the nearest comfortable corner, my husband knows that his social time will soon come to a close. This is in large part because mine has. I may have learned the tricks to surviving required social situations without looking like too much of a spaz, but I don't particularly enjoy standing in dark corners.

I sure would like to have "The Time of My Life" at the next birthday skating party, but I just don't. (It's harder to stand in a corner in roller skates.) I dream of one day being dramatically rescued by my husband as he declares, "C'mon, Tonilyn. 'No one puts Baby in a corner.'"

I distinctly feel like a geeky 1980s movie social reject telling Michael I'm ready to abandon the "fun" social mayhem. I try to stay in my corner for as long as I can, thereby giving my husband as much time as possible to enjoy his social spotlight.

Seriously, there are only so many times a person can google Han Solo to see if he has a Twitter page and only so many rounds of Angry Birds a person can play before getting angry at the birds. Really, though, I'm avoiding asking the question that all social butterflies dread, "Can we go now?"

"Honey, can we go now?"

The look on his face is heartbreaking—and I'm the cause. I'm not sure which is more uncomfortable—asking my husband to leave or asking myself to stay. Asking Michael to leave a party is like asking a five-year-old to abandon Disneyland to go eat dinner at a tofu bar. This is the point of the evening when my husband will now turn into my mother.

As a child, when my sister and I would ask my mom how much longer we'd be shopping at T.J.Maxx, her response was always the same, "Ten more minutes."

Initially, my sister and I believed her. We'd stop bothering her and opt for playing another round of hide-and-seek inside the clothes racks, scaring other lady shoppers and confusing employees. Ten minutes would pass. Fifteen minutes would pass . . .

"Mom, can we go now?"

"Ten more minutes."

Ten sets of ten minutes would go by, and two hours later my sister and I would finally find ourselves home, having missed our *He-Man* and *She-Ra* hour.

"Michael, can we go now?"

"Ten more minutes."

Perhaps if he were looking for the cheapest, greatest Ralph Lauren pantsuit ever, I could cut him some slack.

This quiet moment screams how different we really are.

Most times I think our opposite natures complement one another. I can give my affable husband the phone, and he can talk to the scary telemarketer for me. Michael knows he can depend on my amazing listening skills in order to remember important conversations word for word.

"Tonilyn, where did you say you put the leftovers?"

"I said I ate the leftovers."

Our differences encourage our closeness. But this introvert vs. extrovert debacle is one instance when I wish he were more like me. This wish does not breed a deeper acceptance of my man and is not very sportsmanlike of me, but if we were alike, we'd be able to understand each other more instead of being at odds. If he were more of an introvert, staying in wouldn't be a big deal at all. He'd stay home and enjoy a good *Grease 2* marathon as much as I did.

I'd bet money that Michael wishes his wife had an outgoing loud streak hiding deep within her. If I were more chatty, I'd be out every night with my husband engaging in witty banter. What a team we'd be! We'd be like an old 1940s black-and-white movie couple. (Maybe I could get some great heels and an even better hat?)

Sadly, my husband and I are a constant social (or antisocial) disappointment to each other.

I thought maybe I could avoid this personality discrepancy altogether by simply avoiding it altogether. If I saw a crowded concert looming in the distance on our calendar, I came up with a plethora of almost-legitimate excuses not to attend. I figured, if Michael went out on his own, he'd have more fun. He could certainly stay longer than seventeen minutes and twenty-four seconds—give or take a few milliseconds.

"So, I think you should just go without me. I really have to write."

"So, I think you should just go without me. I'm really tired."

"So, I think you should just go without me. I really have to wash my hair."

So, I think I have to come up with better excuses.

"Come with me," was Michael's request each time I told him I was staying home.

Every time I bagged on going out, Michael became more frustrated. He didn't understand why anyone would pass up a fun social hour—or seven. I thought he'd be happy to go out and feed his inner party animal as long as he wanted. I thought surely this plan of action would release some tension, and we'd both get what we wanted. Apparently, my husband wanted me with him.

"Why won't you come with me?" he asked after I deftly tried to avoid a dinner by telling him my nails took all night to dry.

"I just don't like going out as much as you do," I grimaced. "You'll have more fun without me."

"But I won't. I want you to be there."

His body language spoke louder than his words. I recognized the defensive tone and the vulnerable stare. Michael was taking my decision personally. My choice to stay at home said to him, "You aren't a good enough reason for me to want to go out."

If my husband had even a tiny shy bone in his body, he'd know why I wilt in certain social situations. He would know how large crowds overwhelm me and how confined and awkward I feel at parties. I had to make him understand. If he understood, then he wouldn't be disappointed. I tried to explain. I tried telling him I loved spending time with him—alone. I tried using language he'd understand . . .

"When I'm at a party or a concert for a long time, I feel like a Cowboys fan at a Redskins game."

"A Cowboys fan would never go to a Redskins game."

You would have thought by now I could have mastered the art of the football analogy.

It is so important to Michael that I share in his social hour with him that when I opt out of the social hour, he opts out of a good mood. I love the fact that my husband wants to share everything with me, but I never knew he'd want to share his party time too.

When I decide to go to a party (against my better judgment), I feel even more uncomfortable than normal. I watch the digital minutes tick slowly on my phone. I challenge myself to wait as long as I can before I ask to leave or eat another brownie. If I stay at home, I make my husband unhappy, and if I stay at a party, I make me unhappy. I'm in a tight spot.

I've often wondered what it would be like not to be me—to be more outgoing. I watch my tall blonde social butterfly of a husband flitting from group to group, and wonder what it would be like to be him. I'm fairly certain that my husband never wonders what it would be like to be me. (He does wonder what it might be like to have breasts, but I don't think that's the same thing.) My awkward and shy behavior remains foreign to him, and that just makes me feel like more of a social loser.

I did understand one thing. My husband wanted me to share in whatever social experience he had planned. This was important to him. So, since it was clear neither of us were changing what's inherent within us, I compromised with myself.

Secretly, I decided upon a happy medium. That's fair, right? I'd go out half of the time. The other half of the time I'd devote to nail drying or hair washing. It was the only option that I could come up with without trying to change my husband—or myself.

"Come with me?"

"Sure, I'll go tonight," I said, knowing tomorrow night I'd be able to finish my book on the couch at home.

Michael's face lit up.

My husband was so excited to have me with him at a social event, he never let go of my hand. My fingers turned a little blue. (They matched my nail polish.) When I was out of atypical weather systems to discuss, I started scoping out a quiet corner and tried sneaking away. My fingers stayed tightly gripped in my husband's hand. He wouldn't let go.

I started to panic. I had nothing left to talk about. I had no other uninteresting topics to bring up. That's when I noticed, my husband was prompting me.

"Tonilyn, what did you think of the movie we saw yesterday?"

"What?! I . . . um . . . uh . . . " Wait, this was something we'd chatted about at great length yesterday. I could answer this question.

And the prompts kept coming.

As I stood there in the middle of the room, I realized I was actually talking. I was actually engaging in conversations. Michael accomplished what a whole four pack of Bartles & Jaymes never could.

For another nine minutes, I felt like my husband. I was outgoing. That night the corner remained empty except for the shy dust bunnies that lurked there marveling at my brilliant conversational skills.

My whole party-going life, I had felt alone. I was lost in a conversational abyss never to return. With my husband's support, I can stand in the center of the room. I don't feel as awkward because I have finally found my perfect wingman—at a party and in life. It's certainly quite a feat keeping Baby out of her safe, dark corner, but my husband has found a way.

Now, if he could just find a way to stop those dessert table brownies from spontaneously popping into my mouth.

CHAPTER 28

A Woman's Work Is Done

Finding teamwork in your marriage

Ellen and Frank

I can hear the vacuum running upstairs. Even though the noise is loud, I find the pattern strangely comforting—back and forth, back and forth, back and forth, back and left. *Wait! What is he doing?* He knows that in order to get up all the dog hair you have to follow the same path at least four times! Over twenty-five years of vacuuming experience qualifies me as a cleaning expert in this instance. Ready to walk upstairs to remind him of this, I remember our deal.

I sit back down.

Frank can handle it.

If I go upstairs and start vacuuming (the right way), I know me well enough to know that I will get sucked into vacuuming for the rest of my life. My two girls will have to bury me with that monstrous dirt sucker, and I don't think they make caskets big enough for a wife and her trusty vacuum. My husband is *trying* to be a good housewife. I'm trying to let him.

It only took me a quarter of a century to even consider shirking all of my wifely chores and cut a deal with Frank—that and my much-older-than-a-quarter-of-a-century back going out. All professionals retire at some point—even professional wives. However, listening to the nightmarishly uneven roar drowning out HGTV makes me question my decision.

My husband and I have different cleaning styles, so listening to his less-clean style above me is hard for me to take. Where I happily bring out the bleach and rubber gloves to decontaminate the bathroom sinks, my husband chooses a simple sponge and Tilex. Years of trying to keep Jenny and Amy germ-free has elevated my cleaning standards to unattainable heights. But can something ever be *too* clean? Can a bed ever be *too* made? I don't think so.

Until very recently, taking care of the house has always been my job. As a self-avowed card-carrying Super Mom/Super Wife, I gave myself no wriggle room when it came to my self-assigned chores.

Frank's crazy 6 a.m.-to whenever schedule never allowed him to participate in much of a set schedule/cleaning schedule/cooking schedule/schedule schedule, so I made one up that involved Frank helping with non-scheduled things like carrying laundry to the laundry room or putting dishes in the dishwasher and a possible late-night-after-play-rehearsals chauffeuring gig. This schedule lasted until Jenny went to college and Amy was in high school.

With the girls all grown up, I went back to work part-time. Even then, I made my Super Mom/Super Wife schedule work. I never cut myself an ounce of Super Mom/Super Wife slack (except once when I had the stomach flu). The good mom and wife in me couldn't be stopped—which meant that I did everything that I'd always done before going to work in the afternoons.

On days I worked, Amy came home to find her laundry folded, and Frank came home to his dinner prepared. Even though I suppose Amy and Frank are old enough to fix their own dinner and fold their own laundry, in my mind that didn't mean they *should* or *could*. (Amy can't fold her shirts thin enough to fit in her drawers properly, and Frank can't make Amy's favorite chicken dinner as well as I can.)

If I didn't do my homework, Amy's clothes would never see the inside of her closet (only her bedroom floor), and Frank would overcook enough chicken to refill a chicken coop. If I didn't keep up the care and feeding of my family, who would?

I couldn't give up being a wife and a mother just because I was going back to work—Amy might never wear clean underwear again! My husband and daughter might suffer severe bouts of food poisoning! I *could* make it work.

And I did.

Until Amy went to college.

I cannot believe I'm actually sitting here listening to the running vacuum cleaner run amuck upstairs. My lovely back-and-forth system is totally unrecognizable—back and right, back further and left, right and diagonal. I hope the carpet doesn't feel neglected. I may have to go refold some hand towels just to keep my mind off the bedlam above me.

During my busiest laundry, cooking, and carpooling days, I'd longed for the day I could lounge on the sofa sipping my Diet Coke while my husband did all my daily chores. That day has come. As much as I want to *carpe* the *diem* and honor our arrangement, I want to *carpe* the vacuum more. All I've ever wanted (besides my kids to be happy) is for Frank to help out, and now that he is, why in the world can't I let him?

In the past, whenever I asked Frank to help, our conversations went something like this:

"Frank, could you vacuum tonight?"

"Sure! If I have time . . ."

With two busy little girls dancing around the house, I didn't have the time to find out if Frank had the time. My girls needed me to be on top of things for their lives to run smoothly. But now that my nest is empty (except for my husband), I figured a little shirking might be in order.

My twenty-five-year-old schedule may be a little outdated. It might be time for a schedule makeover. Between driving the kids to rehearsals, and the mall, and Baskin-Robbins, I had understood that it was easier for me to get stuff done because I was home more than Frank. Now, that's just not the case.

I was amazed at how quiet the house was with Jenny and Amy out of it. After watching the Home Shopping Network for a full month straight, I thought that it might be a good idea if I went back to work. The Home Shopping Operators were starting recognize my voice when I called, "Ellen, is that you? That genuine Diamonique ring is quite a deal today isn't it?" I wasn't sure if that was a good thing.

The twenty boxes of HSN goodies stacked in my dining room made me think that I might need something else to do with my time. My part-time job turned into a full-time job (with evening hours), and now Frank and I are both forty-hours-a-weekers. That's when the rebellious, responsibility-shirking dreams started sneaking around loudly in my head. After getting home after eleven at night, pulling myself out of bed about 12:30 in the afternoon, folding things, vacuuming dog hair, only to precook a dinner I wasn't even going to be around to eat—I was exhausted.

It seemed silly for me to continue my mom itinerary with no kids in the house. Frank lives here too. He knows how to vacuum.

"Frank, would you mind helping me vacuum?"

A younger Frank might have scoffed or pouted, but an older, wiser Frank simply asked, "Why?"

A younger Ellen might have been insulted, but an older, wiser, more beautiful Ellen used her explaining-to-her-husband voice and explained, "I'm just too tired to do it all."

Younger and older Frank responded together with their normal, "Sure! If I have time . . ."

Like a sage husband, he found the time, because an older, wiser Frank knows not to argue with a tired, cranky, older Ellen. She has no problem instating cleaning incentives like gathering clumps of dust and putting them on her husband's head while he sleeps.

Still, I didn't realize that the vacuum cleaner havoc upstairs would be its own form of wifely torture. I suppose I could sneak up there when Frank's asleep and run the vacuum quietly. He certainly wouldn't hear it going over his snoring, but next week he'd see the checkerboard pattern, and he'd know.

I can let Frank vacuum.

I can let Frank vacuum.

I can let Frank vacuum while I wait for the chicken to be done—the chicken Frank put in the oven almost fifteen minutes ago. (I hope he set the oven to 350 not 250 again. Funny thing about me, I like my chicken cooked.)

Vacuuming is just the next step in a long line of household chores I've given (tried to give) over to my husband. Recently, I had passed my iron skillet over to Frank.

"Frank, do you think you could start cooking dinner?"

"Why?"

Again using my explaining-to-my-husband voice I explained, "I'm not home to eat anyway . . ."

Logic won the day—or Frank's hunger.

I've relinquished my Lady of the House crown to my husband along with my "World's Best Mom" cooking apron. (The apron really brings out his eyes.) I never thought about *how* Frank would take over. I just wished that he would. I didn't know that Frank would be doing everything wrong.

In the beginning of our marriage, I cared too much what Frank and his family thought. I wanted to be the perfect mother and wife. I took pride in what the house looked like for my kids. But times have changed, and Frank and I need to change along with them. I need to let go and let Frank. The wife/mom in me is having a hard time letting go. I wonder if the kitchen towels need refolding?

I know that my husband will never be able to Pledge the coffee table like I can, but I keep telling myself that it's okay—a lot. When the kids left the house, some of that Super Mom pressure went with them, and I don't feel quite so anxious when life isn't swept and buffed. I don't have to be perfect anymore.

What started out as Frank vacuuming here and there, and only cooking during the weekdays, has evolved into Frank vacuuming all the time and cooking for me too. Flipping through TV channels only to hear someone else tell me, "Dinner's ready," is a whole new experience—a nice experience. If the laundry sits on the dryer for a couple of days, then so be it. If I come home to smelly chicken—oh well. I'll just order a pizza instead.

I have a deal with my husband.

I took care of the house for the first twenty-five years of our marriage, now Frank can take care of it for the second twenty-five. After that, I've promised Frank I'll take over again. Frank jokes that it seems like a pretty good deal. And I still lend a hand here and there. (When I can stand it no further. If a wife vacuums and no one is around to hear it, did she really vacuum? I'm not telling.)

After twenty-five years, my back and I deserve a little break—which is why I'm going to sit here on the couch and listen to the uneven roar of the vacuum upstairs.

I could get used to this.

Thanks to Frank, I'll have twenty-five years to try.

CHAPTER 29

The One That I Want

Finding your best self through the support of your partner

Christine and Danny

I think Danny is speaking another language because it sounds like he just told me to quit my job.

For the most part, I'm pretty good at understanding him even over the dinner he happens to be chewing right now. There aren't too many occasions when I have to get out my Danny-to-Christine translation guide. And during the times when we aren't speaking one another's language, once I translate his-speak to her-speak, I'm a pro at finding the slip up and getting us back on track.

In this case, I know I'm going to have to abandon our manual because it's going to be of zero help to me here. I think Danny is saying, "You can quit your job," and it's the middle word with which I'm having a problem. I can't seem to find it in my translation guide or in my own personal mental dictionary—at least not the way Danny is using it.

I stare at my iced tea and think about that bizarro middle word. It would make more sense to me if it were used in a sentence like "Christine, *quit* eating all of that pie." That I get. Otherwise, I don't grasp its usage. I know Danny's not saying that I should *leave* my job.

How is it supportive to tell your partner to *leave* a job? I know we don't always see eye-to-eye on everything (especially when it comes to music), but I'm confused by the kind of encouragement he's offering me now.

In our relationship, we try (even if we don't always succeed) to listen to one another. I think Danny's been listening a bit too closely. Danny is merely taking my venting too seriously. That must be it. Everyone gripes about their job.

I watch Danny feed the dog his carrots and think what else do people talk about at dinner if they aren't grumbling about their irksome coworker or their annoying blonde boss who takes credit for all of their hard work? Complaining about a job is a universal theme like love and hate and pie. Everyone goes through stuff at work, don't they?

Danny knows full well I'm not a quitter of jobs or anything else—but especially not of jobs. I work at things. I work at it until I make it work. So what if I have to sacrifice some of my sanity in the process? That's just the price you pay when you want to be successful. That's what mature working-place adults do. That's what my family does.

No one in my family has ever *left* a job. Even the mere thought makes me shudder with irresponsibility. What would my parents think? Would my dad stop talking to me altogether? In a hushed whisper to all her friends, would my mom start referring to me as "the creative one"?

My parents picked one job and worked it for thirty years. We do not abandon our posts. We stick with it for life—even if we hate it.

"You can do whatever you want . . . ." The strange untranslatable sentences continue to pour out of Danny's mouth in between sips of soda. I'm guessing he doesn't mean I should go audition for *Dancing with the Stars*.

"Danny, I can't leave my job," I plunk my fork down decidedly. How come each time Danny suggests I should leave the light-headedness in my skull builds, and I resort to such mature actions like "fork plunking"?

"Why not? You keep saying you want to be more fulfilled, and you know that job isn't it."

My job is not my calling. I know that. Danny knows that. It wasn't even supposed to be a permanent position. When I interviewed, I just needed a temporary job until I could figure out what kind of real job I wanted.

A friend suggested that I come to her office and interview because an executive assistant was going out on maternity leave. Since it was only supposed to be a couple of months, I thought I'd give it a try. I could handle anything for two or three months until I figured out what I really wanted to do with the rest of my life. Then the woman I replaced couldn't leave her new baby to come back to her old job, so what was originally to be three months turned into a year. And then a year suddenly turned into ten. Ten years I've been there.

I didn't mind the job so much in the beginning. I was dealing with data entry and that was really satisfying to a certain part of my detail-oriented brain. What the job doesn't satisfy is me. There's nothing at all creative about what I do. (The smiley faces I add to spreadsheets don't count.) I come home crabby and exhausted. Between the office drama and the cold computer, my soul gets sucked out of my body every time I sit down at my desk.

"There's more to life—you are capable and creative," his pep talk continued as he continues to feed the dog his vegetables.

Capable and creative at what? Quitting?

Danny's constant *leaving* suggestion makes me dizzy—that's after the nausea finds its place in my stomach. I know Danny sees it. There's no way he could miss it—my workplace anxiety. It makes our dinners less enjoyable, but my queasy stomach does keep me from overeating. Granted, not the best dieting plan. It probably doesn't help that I'm not very quiet about the frustration that follows me home. In fact, my work horror stories contain as much detail as my accounting graphs.

Danny may think my stories are too long, but I find it important to paint a clear picture of what I must endure there day in and day out. Knowing what color shoes I happened to be wearing or what kind of sandwich I was eating while the exasperating encounter took place are crucial details. If I can't be creative at work, at least I can be creative in my storytelling.

My artistic expression of workplace life is as much for Danny as it is for me. If I were a dancer, I could "dance it out," but I'm not so I opt for words instead of spellbinding movement. I use many colorful words to spin the many different ways that my boss is taking credit for my work.

When my boss and I are called into meetings with our department heads, my giving boss gives herself all the credit for all the work that she didn't do. All this stealing of thunder happens right in front of me. (I've heard it happens behind me too.) Listening to the powers-that-be congratulate her on a job well done makes me want to give her my two-second notice. (She doesn't deserve two weeks.)

I may hate my job, but I am good at it. I take pride in it. If I'm going to do it, I'm going to do it right. That's just the way I am. That's how my parents raised me. I wish my parents had raised my boss, because she does not operate with the same manifesto.

I hate what she's doing. But if I confront her who knows what she might do. She'll likely fire me. On the surface, that might seem like the best of both worlds. I could go all smart like Melanie Griffith in *Working Girl* and tell my boss off in the most satisfying way possible while secretly having taken all of her clients. That would be a good day with an incredibly detailed story to tell.

For that to happen, I think I need to hire a good scriptwriter. I know there's no way I would do any of that on my own. She's my boss. What if she really did fire me? My family does not get fired. Ever. Realistically, what am I supposed to do?

According to Danny, I'm supposed to quit.

"Danny, seriously I can't quit. How will I make any money?" I say as I take my unfinished plate of chicken into the kitchen.

Danny raised an eyebrow, "What do you value more—money or yourself?"

Both—I think. The fact that I've stayed at this job longer than I ever planned makes me ask myself, "Why?" Fast and quick answers pop up from the dark of my mind. The lazy side of me pipes up quietly and says, "Because it's easier." The practical side steps in and adds, "You make a good living there." Those are the easy answers I repeat like a mantra in the morning while trying to figure out how to call in sick.

I can't just quit—but what's keeping me there? More than that though, how can I turn my back on the way I was raised? My family doesn't leave a good paying job. Everything I believe about work ethic and sticking with it and being a loyal employee is as much a part of me as my legs or arms or the pie I ate for lunch. I can't separate myself from myself, can I?

Danny is giving me an option that I never entertained. He's saying I could leave. He's saying I'm better than this job. He's saying I can find something else that energizes me. Is he right?

What would it feel like to (gulp) quit? Why am I working so hard to advance in a career that I don't care about at all? It's like I'm expending all my energy pushing on a door that says "pull." It's a futile task, and I don't even want to go into the next room anyway! I've been pushing against this closed door for so long, I've gotten good at it. I'm comfortable with it. What would it feel like to stop pushing?

Scraping the food off of my plate into the sink, I think (and tune out the Tom Waits song that has just randomized itself to the front of the iPad playlist): I can feel my unhappiness. I know I'm frustrated. But being happy doing my job never really occurred to me—until Danny spoke up.

Danny has always been invested in making the most out of life. I see that in him, and I guess he can see that in me. I find it crazy that my partner is able to see a strength in me that I find hard to conjure. That fire he sees must be hiding in there somewhere. I wouldn't feel such a sense of injustice when I'm mistreated at work, if it wasn't stoking down deep. It's just trying to channel that strength so I can take action—an action that would be so against what I thought I wanted. There are times when I envy Danny's certainty, and this is one of them.

Danny has a strong sense of self. I see him speaking out when he's mistreated—a situation where I often chose to retreat. I want to stay nice. I want to stay good. Danny just wants to stay himself.

"Christine, you do not have to be defined by your job," Danny adds as he and the dog follow me into the kitchen.

"It's just I don't have anything lined up . . ."

I hear myself making excuse after excuse every time my partner utters a supportive sentence. Each time I defend my choice to stay, I feel a little weaker inside. I feel myself sidestepping my inner strength and pushing it back down there to wait.

Wait for what?

Ten more years to go by?

Danny believes I can do it. He thinks that I can find a job that I love (or at least tolerate). He has known all along what I really want to do. I really want to quit.

I want to be fulfilled creatively at a job where people appreciate me. I've always wanted that, but somewhere along the line I settled. Quitting this horrid job would allow me the freedom to be the person I want to be—a strong person who stands up for what she wants. The fact that he can see that courageousness in me, is helping me to see it in myself.

Maybe I can quit.

Maybe with Danny's help, I can do this.

I'm not going to march into work tomorrow and give my two-second notice, but I think that I can entertain the idea that being a quitter might be the best decision I've ever made. Danny's unwavering faith in me is helping me take that risk. I love having a partner who encourages me to be true to myself and follow my heart when my fear dismisses it.

My partner is here to back me up when I need it, and his constant support in me shows me everyday why he's the one that I want.

CHAPTER 30

Move Over Sally Field

Finding unconditional love

Sophie and Nick

There's a stranger in my house. I should be terrified. I watch the news, so I know strangers aren't safe. Strangers hand out Halloween candy all year long and should be avoided at all costs. Walking through my house, I hear the occasional muffled cackle. I can make out light dancing steps pirouetting down the hall. I should probably run for my life, or at least call someone. Then in a fit of hysterical giggles I remember—it's me. The stranger in my house is me. I don't recognize myself—and neither does my husband.

Over the last year I've lost a lot. I've lost pounds and dress sizes and years of insecurities. I hope these things are truly lost, never to return again, like my 1980s self-inflicted Rod Stewart haircut and my acid-wash jeans. It's taken a whole lot of sweating and even more dessert skipping, but I've lost 100 pounds.

Wait.

Let me rephrase.

"I HAVE LOST ONE HUNDRED POUNDS!" she exclaimed shouting and jumping up and down!

This explains the down-the-hall-pirouettes and random giggle fits. I can't believe I'm me!

Now I know how superheroes feel when they discover they have a crazy special power. My superpower isn't as awesome as seeing through walls or as cool as scaling buildings in spandex. (Although wearing spandex is now an option.) Mine is more subtle but just as noteworthy—I know who I am. I've finally met me.

It's an unbelievably spectacular feeling—sensing the real me rising to the surface. I just want to give this new Sophie room to twirl and dance until she collapses in hysterical giggles or needs to take a Dramamine for excessive spinning.

I adore New Sophie's zest for life and fearless attitude! I'm so ready to follow New Sophie to the ends of the earth—or at the very least to her next spin class. However, I'm not so sure I can get my husband to follow her into the next room.

New Sophie, complete with Twirling Action, is puzzling to my non-twirling husband. Nick has never met this version of me. Truth be told, neither have I. I'm getting used to her just like he is. These skinnier days my husband looks at me like he's looking at a stranger.

Walking down our hall, Nick is never sure which Sophie he's going to meet. Will he see old Sophie trudging around in her PJs, always ready for a night in? Or will he come across new confident Sophie sporting her size 6 dress, complete with glass of chardonnay and *Sex and the City* stilettos, ready for a night out? More often than not, it's the party animal version of Nick's wife he's been running into these days.

"Nick! Let's go out and do something fun after dinner, okay?"

"Um . . . no that's okay—you go ahead."

Our evenings together used to consist of dinner and a movie—at home. All. The. Time. Now, I want to conquer the world! Nick wants to conquer the remote control.

While my husband hangs at home, I'm out there getting into trouble and loving it. Not the kind of trouble that would land me overnight in jail, thus propelling me to write my memoirs at an early age. Nope, just the kind of trouble where men gawk and trip over my newfound confidence (and red platform shoes), thus propelling these men's wives to shoot "You did not just check her out in front of me" looks at them.

I thought that my husband would be tripping along with the best of them. I waited anxiously for the tripping and gawking phase of our relationship to begin.

As more and more weight started coming off, I waited for Nick to whisk his new hot wife away to exotic places like Florence, Italy, or Cincinnati, Ohio. There's been nary a whisk—except, of course, the one that sits in our kitchen.

Nick hasn't said much about my transformation—not that he ever says much about anything really. I'm wondering if my newfound *joie de vivre* (and use of French phrases) is silencing him even more. Am I frightening my husband?

Over the last months, I've been expecting him to say *something* about this new me emerging from the shadows. I was hoping for things like "Sweetie, you seem so happy," or "Sweetie, you look phenomenal," or "Sweetie, let's go out." If he loved me, he'd say *something*.

"Nick, let's go out after dinner tonight?!"

"No thanks."

If he loved, me he'd say something.

"Nick, what if we just went to a movie?!"

"No thanks."

If he loved me, he'd say something.

"Nick, how about we just take a walk around the neighborhood?!"

"No thanks."

If he loved me, he'd say something.

"Sophie, this asparagus is amazing."

If he loved me, he'd say something else.

I'm sure Nick thought I'd always stay the same couch-loving girl that he married—I sure did. Maybe I've changed too much. Maybe Nick is fed up with New Sophie. Maybe he's fed up with all the fancy twirling. What if I'm changing myself right out of my marriage?

"We just changed . . ."

That's the first thing I hear.

When my divorced friends tell me why they have decided to separate, they crinkle their lips into a timid smirk and say, "We just changed." This is their go-to phrase. For me, it seems to encompass a multitude of sins. Where's their commitment? Where's their love? I think to myself, "A person can't change *that* much."

I told myself I'd never sit where these friends sit. My husband and I have committed to each other for forever. There's no way I'd change myself out of our marriage.

And then I'm reminded of my grand leaps down the hall where once there were little steps, and my cackling laugh where once there was a retiring giggle.

I'm no longer the same girl my husband married. Not even close. I can only imagine how bizarre this must be for Nick. The woman he fell in love with is not the same woman standing in the kitchen cooking multigrain pasta and skipping the chocolate dessert. (I don't always skip the chocolate dessert. Some things remain the same.)

I'm skinnier now than when we got married. If Nick liked this new me, he'd be gushing all over his hot new wife, right? There'd be rose petals living perpetually on our bed, and Nick would install a new red carpet down the hall just for me. I feel the change happening between us. Nick is mistaking my confidence for arrogance. I can feel it.

If he loved me, he'd say something.

Maybe he doesn't love me.

What if my change is way too much to handle? I always assumed that as a couple Nick and I would continue to grow and change together, but that was before we were even a couple. I've come to realize that role playing with Barbie and Ken as a tween does not help you solve complex marital problems. (Barbie does help one color coordinate polyester outfits with plastic heels, but that is a very specific skill set not applicable here.)

I'm feeling the most confident I've ever felt in my entire life. Why then am I feeling the most insecure I've ever felt in my marriage?

What if Old Nick really doesn't like New Sophie? What if that's the reason he doesn't want to go out with me? What if that's the reason he doesn't tell me how great I look? Or how happy I seem? Or how beautiful I am? What if he loves Old Sophie more than me?

What if my husband doesn't love me?

Even the mere thought sends a jolt to my stomach. Who knew diet and exercise could change so much more than my waistline? It was time to go fishing . . .

"Why do you love me?"

Yep, I was fishing. Fishing for the truth and perhaps some reassurance. I needed to know if my husband was still with me, and asking was the quickest way to find out.

"Why do you love me?"

Nick's eyes glaze over. It's like I've asked him to mow the lawn.

"Because I do . . ." is his brief answer.

How is that any kind of answer?!

I love you because . . . you are my everything. A proper answer.

I love you because . . . your eyes sing to my soul. A poetic answer.

I love you because . . . you are beautiful. A real answer.

Those are answers! I want one of those! I want some real reasons! I at least want a complete sentence!

I stand there in my new skin feeling broken. Everything I thought I'd fixed feels cracked and sagging. I am a new, beautiful version of me, so why isn't my husband fawning all over me like all my friends? Even the teenage barista in Starbucks winks at me!

My friends (and teenage baristas) have nothing but wonderful, encouraging things to say about my commitment to weight loss. But my husband is treating me like he always has. Nothing new. Nothing different—even though I am. Nick should love me more just because I do.

Maybe if Nick could just tell me *why* he loves me, then I would *know* he loves me. I'll ask him again. I just need to pick my moment . . .

"Sweetheart, this asparagus is amazing . . ."

"Why do you love me?"

Maybe not the best moment.

Ignoring the jolts of lightning in my stomach, I wait for Nick to respond. If he could just give me a solid answer—an answer that could help make sense of it all.

"I love you, because I love you."

I stare at him and try to follow his man-logic. "I love you, because I love you?" What does that really mean? *I love you because I love you?* The lightning storm in my stomach eases, and I wonder why. Is this his final answer?

I'm skeptical, but I accept Nick's answer because he looks me straight in eye and totally believes what he tells me. I can't argue with conviction like that.

I clear the dinner plates and begin to think about our marriage—the little things. The good things.

Last week, I finally got Nick to go out dancing with me. Although he didn't dance a step, he went with me and held my purse the whole evening. Not many men would stand in a crowded club, house music blaring, holding their wife's purple clutch. Does my husband love me?

The next day, we were still in hysterics about the bartender's hat choice. It was so strange even my husband noticed. We still laugh together. Does my husband love me?

"Nick, what did the green grape say to the purple grape?"

"I don't know, Sweetheart."

"Breathe, idiot! BREATHE!"

He laughed.

My husband loves me.

Through this whole process, Nick had always seen me. His love for me never changed like mine did for myself. Thin, fat, or with eggplant highlights, Nick loves me for who I am. I don't have to knock myself out trying to get him to love New Sophie. Because my husband loves *me*. That's what "I love you, because I love you" means. Man-logic—so elegant in its simplicity sometimes.

Wait.

Let me rephrase.

MY HUSBAND LOVES ME! HE REALLY *REALLY* LOVES ME!

Eat your heart out, Sally Field.

→HUSBAND RAISING 101←

It's truly an amazing feeling, confidently knowing that Nick loves me no matter what. My husband loves me. He loves me! He really loves me!

—**Sophie on unconditional love**

What wife doesn't want to be truly loved for herself? What husband doesn't want to be accepted for who he is? Unconditional love—a popular literary topic. Authors and poets from the beginning of time have sought to capture this ardor. They are not alone in their quest—so do everyday wives and their husbands.

Lily realized that it's the differences in her marriage (not her cold heart) that make it unique. Ellen discovered what it means to truly be a team. Tonilyn recognized that unconditional love plays a part in brownie eating. Chloe and Christine felt how much their husbands truly believed in them. And Sophie finally realized that her husband has always loved her for who she is on the inside and not on the scale. In each instance, our couples were able to take their real problems, uncover the core issues, and find out that true love and support during trying times bring out the best in us.

Because honestly, who doesn't need to be raised up every now and then?

SKILL BUILDING COVERED IN PART IV

- ☐ How to establish a true give-and-take in your relationship in order to achieve balance in your marriage
- ☐ How to bring out the best in your partner
- ☐ How to make small talk at parties
- ☐ What true commitment in marriage means
- ☐ How to cultivate a deeper understanding of unconditional love

AFTERWORD

Hello, there. Welcome to the afterword to *How to Raise a Husband*. I mention the title because I want you to be sure I know what it is. You see, I am the husband. My beautiful bride may have written this tome, but I, in my infinite humble objectivity, plainly see that *How to Raise a Husband* exists only because of me.

It's not that I was a terrible, untamed person or some socially inept hermit, capable of communicating by only uttering favorite lines from *Star Wars*. (No, not at all—I also used lines from *Star TREK*.) You see, I was a very capable, intelligent, reasonably grounded, moral, happy, successful guy who had been through things and learned from them. I didn't think I was any more in need of "raising" than any of us. I have found, though, as with any good, purposeful relationship, that I became a better me through knowing my wife, and she recognized that.

My smart wife has a knack for reading people. She naturally looks at what makes people tick, and she has the talent for clearly seeing what helps people—and what's not working for someone, too. And, probably most important and most remarkable, when she sees that, rather than instantly pointing it out like some dogmatic life coach, she stands back, intuiting that people really only learn when they see it for themselves.

I made some poor choices earlier in our relationship. She could see it as it was happening, yet she didn't say so. She patiently looked on, watching me with love and understanding, waiting to see if I would clue in or not. (Luckily, I did.) If she had been there saying it all along, trying to *teach* me or *fix* me, it would have pushed me away. I know myself enough to know I would have told her (and myself) that she was way too controlling and really didn't know anything about the perfectly excellent and awesome person I obviously was . . . and then gone on making the same mistakes. But, thankfully, she didn't do that. She just genuinely gets that while she understands what someone might be doing to get in the way of his or her happiness, it's not her place to say so.

So she's more surprised than anyone to find herself writing this book. Telling people how to live is simply not in her nature. Being of service is in her nature, though. So, once the ideas started to flow, she followed where they led. Now that you've read it, you can probably understand and be thankful for the purpose of this book: my wife's desire to help add to the happiness of your life.

So, I just wanted you to know that I, the titular Husband, know what she's been up to with this book. And, I'm deeply thankful for it. My relationship with this woman has helped "raise" me to find the truth in myself and in us. I can say that when I look at the truth, when I strip away the filters of expectation, judgment, and ego and really look, I see my wife, and she's the most beautiful thing I'll ever see. As I said at our wedding, my bride helped me see my true self. And when I did, I saw that what I am is love for her.

My wife knows that feeling and would love it if you did, too.

—MICHAEL, Tonilyn's husband

Acknowledgments

First and foremost, I wouldn't be here without the help of the wives, their husbands, and their stories. (Really, if I'm going to get technical, I wouldn't be here without my parents hooking up, but I will get to that.) I came to these women, my friends, with a crazy idea, and they did not hesitate to jump on board. I thank them for hours and hours on the phone, answering questions, and trusting me with all of their marital secrets. Their honesty made this book come to life. Thanks, ladies. You know who you are, I know who you are, and I thank you for helping me make a dream come true.

To my writing teacher: Thanks for telling me that what was inside of me was worth revealing and for always encouraging me to "dig deeper."

To my supportive friends (you know who you are because I e-mailed you): Thank you, thank you, thank you!

To my professional proofreaders and my proofreading friends: You all handled my work with utmost care, and for that I will say, "You all rule. I still owe you lunch." (Except for the one reader I took out to dinner. We're even.)

To my agent: I can't thank you enough for taking a chance on a first-time writer and for not giving up.

To my editor: I trusted you entirely from our first e-mail. Thank you for "getting it" and loving cupcakes as much as I do.

To my family and extended-through-marriage family—especially my mom, my dad, and my sister. From the very beginning (except for you, little sister, but only because you weren't born yet), you have supported me in everything I have wanted to try. Even T-ball, which lasted all of two days. Mom and Dad, without you believing in me, I wouldn't know how to believe in myself. Without you being proud of me already, I wouldn't know how to put myself out there and come back whole. And if for some reason I didn't make it back all together, I always knew I had a safe place to come to home to. And thank you, little sister, for always playing Danny in *Grease* so I could be Sandy. It has helped me in my creative process.

Now, I said earlier there is the reason this book exists—my husband. That is 110 percent true. ("How can something be more than 100 percent?!" I hear you ask, dear husband.) You *are* the reason this book was written, but it's because of your unconditional confidence in me (and your infinite knowledge of punctuation) not because you provide me with good material. (All right, maybe a little bit because you provide me with good material.) Without your self-effacing sense of humor and willingness to be open, this book never would have been. Thank you for your constant support. If not for that, I'd still be sitting in the game room watching the Home Shopping Network. This whole journey wouldn't have the meaning it does if you weren't by my side bringing out the "us" we create every day together.

Thank you Adelade for sitting next to me as I wrote. Thank you Percival for encouraging me to take frequent breaks. Thank you Wynnifred for wanting to write some of this for me. And thank you E simply for being born.

About the Author

Tonilyn hails from a long and distinguished line of married couples. Collectively, Tonilyn's grandparents have been married 112 years while her parents have been married for forty years. She herself has been married over eight years. This wealth of experience gives her a unique perspective—while her husband gives her priceless material.

Tonilyn has always preferred writing in her room to playing kick ball outside. Tonilyn's essays have been published in *True Story Magazine*, *Underwired Magazine*, *Clever Magazine*, *Savvy Women's Magazine*, and *The Florida Times-Union*, Jacksonville. For over three years she was a favorite and featured blogger for *Skirt! National* magazine, and was voted *Skirt*'s second favorite blogger in 2010. Currently she is a blogger for *Pregnancy & Newborn Magazine* (having just had a baby helps). Her collection of essays for *How to Raise a Husband* won the award for Outstanding Nonfiction at the Southern California Writers' Conference.

Before Tonilyn began writing professionally, her life was on the stage. She graduated cum laude with a BFA in musical theater from the Boston Conservatory of Music. She has performed in regional theaters across the country as well as a leading role in a First National Tour. Tonilyn is also a working voice-over artist so when she gets bored she can write her own scripts and record them. Tonilyn lives in LA with her two smart border collies, her one sassy kitty, her one supportive husband, and her one new baby boy. *www.tonilynhornung.com*

To Our Readers

Conari Press, an imprint of Red Wheel/Weiser, publishes books on topics ranging from spirituality, personal growth, and relationships to women's issues, parenting, and social issues. Our mission is to publish quality books that will make a difference in people's lives—how we feel about ourselves and how we relate to one another. We value integrity, compassion, and receptivity, both in the books we publish and in the way we do business.

Our readers are our most important resource, and we appreciate your input, suggestions, and ideas about what you would like to see published.

Visit our website at *www.redwheelweiser.com* to learn about our upcoming books and free downloads, and be sure to go to *www.redwheelweiser.com/newsletter* to sign up for newsletters and exclusive offers.

You can also contact us at *info@rwwbooks.com*.

Conari Press
an imprint of Red Wheel/Weiser, LLC
665 Third Street, Suite 400
San Francisco, CA 94107